Glimmers of Grace

GLIMMERS OF
GRACE

Moments of Peace and Healing
Following Sexual Abuse

FAITH HAKESLEY

Our Sunday Visitor
Huntington, Indiana

Nihil Obstat
Msgr. Michael Heintz, Ph.D.
Censor Librorum

Imprimatur
✠ Kevin C. Rhoades
Bishop of Fort Wayne-South Bend
April 8, 2020

The *Nihil Obstat* and *Imprimatur* are official declarations that a book is free from doctrinal or moral error. It is not implied that those who have granted the *Nihil Obstat* and *Imprimatur* agree with the contents, opinions, or statements expressed.

Except where noted, the Scripture citations used in this work are taken from the *Revised Standard Version of the Bible — Second Catholic Edition* (Ignatius Edition), copyright © 1965, 1966, 2006 National Council of the Churches of Christ in the United States of America. Used by permission. All rights reserved.

Every reasonable effort has been made to determine copyright holders of excerpted materials and to secure permissions as needed. If any copyrighted materials have been inadvertently used in this work without proper credit being given in one form or another, please notify Our Sunday Visitor in writing so that future printings of this work may be corrected accordingly.

Our Sunday Visitor Publishing Division
Our Sunday Visitor, Inc.
200 Noll Plaza
Huntington, IN 46750
1-800-348-2440

ISBN: 978-1-68192-550-9 (Inventory No. T2433)
1. RELIGION—Christian Living—Prayer.
2. RELIGION—Christian Living—Devotional.
3. RELIGION—Christianity—Catholic.

eISBN: 978-1-68192-551-6
LCCN: 2020935625

Cover design: Chelsea Alt
Cover art: Adobe Stock

PRINTED IN THE UNITED STATES OF AMERICA

I dedicate this devotional to you, my dear readers.
To survivors of abuse, for their families, friends, and loved ones:
Please be assured that you are in my daily prayers.
I pray that the Holy Spirit speaks to you in a special way
and that he brings you comfort and healing.

TABLE OF CONTENTS

Introduction 9
What Is a Glimmer of Grace? 17
Recommendations for Use 21

PART I: FINDING GRACE

Acceptance 27
Faith 33
Hope 41
Trust 47
Truth 55
Kindness 63

PART II: FINDING HEALING

Courage 73
Strength 81
Wisdom 87
Perseverance 93
Patience 101
Self-Compassion 109

PART III: FINDING FREEDOM

Gratitude 119
Love 127
Joy 135
Peace 141
Freedom 149

Embracing Grace 157

Embracing a Grateful Heart 159

Acknowledgments 161

Appendix I: A Word on Prayer 163

Appendix II: The Reality of Sexual Grooming 169

Appendix III: Sexual Abuse Resources 173

INTRODUCTION

In my time on this earth, I don't think I've ever done anything that would be considered truly spectacular. I'm no one particularly extraordinary, though I am a beloved child of God. I'm not a saint, although I strive to be one. All too often, my faith feels weak. I'm not famous, and I haven't been blessed with extraordinary book smarts or wit. My talents don't set me apart from the majority of people.

Here's what I have done. By the grace of God and with the support of some very special people, I got through some seemingly impossible hardships and dark times as I grew up, and I have gone on to live a fairly average life. Most people who meet my family and me will tell you that I seem like a perfectly normal woman. But they don't always see what's underneath. Everyone has a story to tell, as do I. The part of my story that inspired this devotional is not a pretty one. It's a story that's uncomfortable to hear, and often difficult for me to tell. There is a certain amount of fear in telling our less-than-glamorous stories — a fear of being judged or ridiculed. Yet, despite all that, the Holy Spirit has given me a tremendous grace in allowing me to be vulnerable enough to share this part of my journey with you, my brothers and sisters in Christ.

So, who am I? For starters, my name is Faith. I am a daughter to the two most wonderful, loving, and supportive parents a girl could ever ask for; a sister; a wife; and a hardworking home-schooling mother. My family strives to live in this confused world but not be a part of it, and my husband and I raise our three children with the ultimate goal of getting one another to heaven one day. That's me in a nutshell. But it might be helpful for you to know a bit more about my background.

I was raised in a loving, Catholic home where the faith was instilled in my three brothers and me from the beginning. We went to Sunday Mass and often weekday Mass; we prayed the Rosary just about every night; we went to confession frequently; and our lives were centered on Christ. I loved the saints and spent a lot of time reading about their lives. That's what I wanted to be: a saint. The life of Saint Thérèse, the Little Flower, had a particular influence on me. She suffered immensely and yet offered up even the smallest trials to God. She called it her "Little Way." She found joy in the smallest, most seemingly mundane situations, and by uniting her suffering to Christ's, she accepted God's grace with openness and love. I wanted to be like her. I wanted to see the bright side and turn to Jesus despite any adversity that might come my way. Little did I know that I would be seeking out inspiration from Saint Thérèse and my other saint friends in my sufferings in the years to come. I was so young, innocent, and naive (as children should be) that I didn't understand right away what it meant to truly suffer. As I got older, the true meaning of suffering entered my life.

When I was fifteen, I got my first job working in my parish rectory. Considering the news stories concerning abuse happening in churches over the past several years, you can probably guess what happened. I experienced months of sexual abuse at the hands of a parish priest. My carefree life came crashing down in front of me. As so often happens to victims of abuse, I blamed myself. I lived in a deep pit of fear, shame, and confusion. I despised myself and began to resent the world around me. My faith wavered because I felt abandoned by my Father in heaven. A part of me felt as though God "let" it happen. During those horrible months, I prayed that the abuse would stop. I prayed that God would preserve my purity and innocence, something that I cherished. I asked "Why?" a lot. I no longer found joy in things I once held dear. I was afraid to tell anyone, even my parents, who had always told us kids to come to them if anyone said or did anything inappropriate. (Sadly, silence typically absorbs victims, since they are embarrassed, blame themselves, and are often fearful of their abusers.) My life became like a deep, dark, silent pit.

A year later, my family and I experienced an indescribably painful loss upon the unexpected death of my oldest brother, Matthew. I found him unconscious on the floor one Sunday morning, and he was pronounced dead a few hours later. The autopsy report showed a heart condition. The grief of Matt's death combined with the trauma of the sexual abuse sent me into a tailspin. Though grief is, of course, normal, my grief went beyond what my parents knew to be normal. Concerned, they put me into grief therapy, and in my very first session, I blurted everything out. I suppose I had reached my limit; the physical, spiritual, and emotional trauma had become too great for one person to bear.

Breaking my silence was one of the greatest graces I have ever received. Being able to get it all out in the open, tell my parents, and eventually see my rapist found guilty, sentenced to prison, and ultimately deported to his native country upon release was a cross to bear. Yet, by the grace of God, and with time, prayer, and patience, I was able to recognize the blessings that accompany suffering. I slowly healed and began to find joy, peace, and, ultimately, freedom.

Healing didn't happen overnight, nor was my faith restored in just a few hours. My journey has often felt long and arduous, but I have been incredibly blessed to meet wonderful people who have helped me along. In 2008, I was given the humbling and life-changing opportunity to meet privately with Pope Benedict

XVI and four other victims of clergy abuse from the Archdiocese of Boston during his visit to Washington, D.C. I can safely say that our meeting is up there at the top of my life's "most profound experiences" list. Although I had wanted to say something heartfelt, when my moment came to speak with the pontiff privately, all I could do was sob. Let me tell you, that was the Holy Spirit speaking, because nothing I could have ever planned would have made such an impact as the most innocent form of expression in that powerful moment. My tears spoke volumes. They spoke for the pain and suffering I had endured as well as all other victims of abuse. The Holy Father appeared to be visibly touched by that meeting, and I ended that day feeling more hope than I had in a very long time. Ever since that moment, I have felt a strong urge deep in my heart to share my story and reach out to others who have experienced not just clergy abuse but any kind of sexual abuse.

Some people hear about the various challenges I have been faced with over the years (rape, death, cancer, a heart condition) and are immediately overcome with sympathy or liken me to Job in the Bible. To me, however, it's just part of my history, a history that has made me who I am today. I have had difficult times, but I attribute my fighting spirit and my ability to overcome adversity to the power of faith and God's tremendous and unfailing grace.

One of the first questions I get from people who are hearing my story for the first time is "Why are you still a Catholic? How have you held on to any faith at all?" That brings me to this book. For many years now, I have been encouraged to reach out to victims of sexual abuse by writing my story. I started writing somewhat blindly, without any real purpose or direction, except simply to tell my story as it happened. Writing was therapeutic, a way for me to put my deepest feelings into words, a way of finding connections between certain events. It has been an opportunity to be completely open, honest, and raw about the hardships I have faced.

As I prayerfully considered how to put this devotional together, I dug deep into my own experiences as a rape victim, as well as the experiences of some of my friends and loved ones, and considered what readers would find helpful. There is a lot of information available about sexual trauma. When I first came forward to a professional therapist, my parents and I felt overwhelmed by all the books, pamphlets, phone numbers, and advice. There was just so much! Thank the good Lord for good (often Christian or Catholic) professionals who were able to guide us, because, otherwise, we wouldn't have known where to begin. The same was true for my husband when he entered the picture several years later and wanted to better understand my past and aid me in my healing.

Sometimes, amid all the statistics, legal definitions, and psychological terms (which can be useful too), we crave a gentle, loving hand to help reassure us that what we are feeling is normal, and a hand to guide us and accompany us on our journey. You, my dear readers, are my inspiration for this devotional, and I write this for you. First and foremost, I want you to know that you are not alone, whether you have been a victim or are reading this because a loved one or a friend has experienced sexual abuse and you are trying to help him or her. Second, no matter where you are in your journey, I want to help you find freedom from the chains that bind you and recognize the gifts that Our Lord is offering you. Third, I want to help each one of you to find your voice and help validate the reality of your experiences, no matter how different they may be from mine. Fourth, I want to encourage you to seek out and accept help when you are ready.

Some trauma survivors may be hesitant to seek out help because they think that it is a sign of weakness. Nothing could be further from the truth! Many important aspects of healing can be provided by professionals who have been specially trained to deal with sexual abuse. The brain is literally altered when a trauma occurs, and there are various therapies (including medication, in some cases) that can help victims overcome distressing symptoms caused by their trauma. This additional assistance can help people move beyond their traumatic experiences so that they can better cope and live more joy-filled and peaceful lives. There are a lot of stigmas associated with trauma, post-traumatic stress disorder

(PTSD), and therapy, but please always remember that there is no shame in seeking help. The fact is, you can pair your faith, prayer, and relationship with God with the help of a professional, and all these things can work together to help you heal.

Remember, healing doesn't happen in a moment. It takes time, patience, trust in God, prayer, and acceptance of his graces and gifts. Healing starts by accepting God's grace to move forward while understanding that not everyone heals in the same way. We are each unique, and God works through each of us in different, sometimes mysterious ways. We never know how our experiences might help and encourage someone else or create positive change in others' lives and in the world. Mother Angelica said, "Everything starts with one person. … I don't care if you're 5 or 105, God from all eternity chose you to be where you are, at this time in history, to change the world."

Being a survivor is not easy. I know what it feels like to be afraid, hopeless, helpless, and alone. My hopelessness one day led me to consider taking away God's most precious gift: my life. I want you to know that you are not alone. There are people out there who understand what you are going through, and God is with you through it all. God's grace is not always something that I feel or understand, and yet without it, I would be nothing. Even in the midst of pain and suffering, he offers his gifts to me; I just have to find the faith and strength to recognize and grasp them.

I want to share with you an event that took place during the writing of this book. In June 2019, I suffered a life-threatening episode of ventricular tachycardia. My ICD (a device inside my body that is capable of correcting most life-threatening irregular heartbeats) fired, saving my life. The shock (no pun intended) of this near-death experience sent me into a deep depression. I suffered from PTSD after the episode and worried almost constantly about the very real possibility that my heart condition could kill me. It's very difficult to describe exactly what takes place in one's mind and heart after an episode like this, except to say that I found myself once again in the all-too-familiar terrain of grief surrounding trauma. For the first time in many years, I returned to psychotherapy with a wonderful Catholic therapist in order to better cope with the varying emotions presenting themselves.

"God is giving you the saint treatment," my pastor told me the day after the episode. All I could think of was, "Well, you know what, God? I don't want this!" However, despite my initial grumbling, God saw fit to use my situation for good, just as he has done with all the other difficulties I have faced. At first, I was convinced that my writing would need to be put on hold, but then someone very wise suggested that maybe God would use my trauma to help me better speak to others in this book. She said that this could be a special opportunity for evangelization firsthand and a special time of growth for me. Here I am, writing about trauma while experiencing a trauma. Although rape and death are certainly different from one another for obvious reasons, all traumas follow varying patterns of grief. As I wrote each reflection, even in my own periods of denial, grief, confusion, and anger, I found myself relating all the more to what I was writing.

Writing a book like this is never easy. I spent much time in prayer and reflection, trying to discern God's will and trying to allow him to write through me. I tried to open my heart and listen, type, and pray that my writing would be divinely inspired. Whether or not it is, I don't know. All I can say is that I was journeying through all the parts of this devotional firsthand, and applying recommendations from my own life. Yes, this book is intended for victims of sexual abuse, but my recent trauma has allowed me to better recall and relate to the sexual trauma I suffered so long ago.

Throughout this process, I have learned so much about myself and my faith and have, more than ever, resigned myself to trust in God's grace, mercy, and love. More and more, I am learning to say, "Jesus, take care of me. You take care of this," instead of trying to figure out all the answers to life's persistent questions myself. Suffering is such a mystery, even to many devout, lifelong Christians. The world's greatest theologian can discuss the reason behind suffering, and yet there still remains that small voice saying,

"But why?"

I am no theologian or philosopher (far from it — philosophy makes my head spin), but I've come to a realization: We live in an imperfect world with sin and suffering, the result of original sin. God sent his only Son to our less-than-perfect world, where he suffered and died for us. For you. For me. For all of us. Because that's how much our Father in heaven loves us. He loves us so much that he was willing to allow his Son to suffer beyond any human comprehension and to die for us, so that one day we could all be with him in heaven and experience more happiness and joy than we can ever imagine. And, just as good came out of Good Friday and we rejoice in the Resurrection on Easter Sunday, God always brings good out of suffering.

God has so many gifts he wants to offer you, some of which I have personally experienced on my journey, and I pray that you will experience the Holy Spirit as you work your way through these reflections. Begin each day by asking him to open your heart and help you relate to each reflection in some way. You will most likely not hear a booming voice from above (I definitely never have), but you will feel gentle beckonings within your heart if you look deep enough and open yourself up to his grace.

You may not always feel Our Lord's presence, but he is united to you on your cross as you journey on the path of healing. There is no one who understands your suffering more than he; no one who suffers right along with you more. Though you may feel as if everything around you is changing and everything is a whirlwind, God never changes; he never leaves your side, even in the midst of all the chaos. If I have learned one thing throughout my life and especially over the course of writing this book, it is to call out to God even at the lowest points in my life. The moment we say yes to God, we open our minds and hearts to his grace. In his most precious hands, he holds out to you his endless gifts and begs you to take them. All you need to do is say yes, and he will work more wonders in your life than you can ever imagine.

WHAT IS A
GLIMMER OF GRACE?

Some of you may be reading the title and wondering, "What exactly does that mean? What's a glimmer of grace anyway?" It's a term inspired by my mom, referring to the little miracles that God sends our way.

I don't know about you, but I've never seen someone raised from the dead or seen a blind person have his or her sight restored by a simple touch. God often sends a different kind of miracle our way — one that doesn't seem profound on the surface and yet causes us to hope, offers us joy and the reassurance of God's love, and fills our minds and hearts with gratitude for God's gifts. We can either ignore these often subtle and quiet glimmers, or, through faith, we can allow them to transform us.

I want to share a little story with you about my experience of a glimmer of grace. My senior year of high school was very difficult. Not only was I still grieving the loss of my brother from a couple of years before, but I was also preparing for a trial at which

I would face my rapist. The thought of having to face him again (and a whole courtroom of strangers) was agony. I spent hours in the district attorney's office as they went over the details of the sexual abuse I had endured and prepped me to testify. All of this was going on as I was struggling to be a normal teenager. My classmates and friends were preparing for graduation and making summer plans. Everyone was excited about the prom and the thought of beginning college in the fall. Me, I felt lucky just to be able to get out of bed in the morning. Because of the stress, my grades were suffering — I had always wanted to be a straight-A student, just like my three brothers — and I experienced frequent fainting spells. Some of my friendships faltered because people were intimidated by what I was going through or didn't know how to treat me or how to talk to me. Without wanting to or meaning to, I pushed people away as well. In short, I felt like a mess.

Around this time, my mom starting encouraging me to look for "glimmers." These, she said, were little rays of light in the darkness. Glimmers are small joys, miracles, and instances in which God speaks to us in ways that sometimes only we can recognize.

The trial began a few weeks after my graduation. On the day I was set to testify, I sat outside the courtroom with the court guard. He was a very nice man, and he chatted away, clearly in an effort to distract me. I nodded and smiled, but that was about all the reaction I could muster. A part of me was trying to pray. Another part of me was mapping out the nearest escape route. With one hand, I gripped the bench I sat on, holding on for dear life. My other hand was in my suit pocket, holding the rosary my mom had given me. All too soon, the guard announced, "Okay, it's time." He opened the door, and I instantly felt as if I were being led to the guillotine.

The guard pressed something into my hand as I passed by him. Surprised, I looked down and saw something small in the palm of my hand. A Tootsie Roll? I was bewildered. Here I was, about to enter a courtroom and testify about being raped, in front of my rapist (a well-liked Catholic priest), strangers, and several people who hated my guts, and this guy was giving me a Tootsie Roll!

At that moment, it hit me — this was one of those glimmers my mom had mentioned. Maybe to most people, that small object in my hand was just a silly Tootsie Roll. However, God used that seemingly meaningless piece of candy to remind me of something greater. The passage from the Gospel of Matthew, chapter 17, about faith the size of a mustard seed suddenly sprang to mind. Even the smallest bit of faith can accomplish great things. All I could think was, "I have to have faith the size of a mustard seed [or a Tootsie Roll, in this case]." It seemed so simple that I almost wanted to laugh.

My heart overflowed with hope and gratitude as my eyes teared up. I looked up and smiled — a genuine smile this time — at that court guard (I didn't even know his name) and whispered, "Thank you." Then I put that Tootsie Roll, that little glimmer of God's grace, into my pocket with my rosary, squared my shoulders, held my head up high, and walked to the front of the room.

God gave me a gift in a moment when I needed it most. Right then, I knew that I would not be alone that day. That Tootsie Roll was my heavenly Father's reminder of his love. It was a sign that he would give me courage and strength to get through the three hours of cross-examination that ensued on the witness stand. I spent that time answering questions openly and honestly, and in difficult moments, I discreetly reached into my pocket and squeezed the little candy. That Tootsie Roll became my greatest comfort.

Those glimmers are what I encourage you to look for every day. God works in mysterious ways, sometimes the most surprising of ways. Allow God to surprise you every day, and allow your heart to be filled with gratitude for his glimmers of grace.

Pause and Pray

Dear Lord,
Help me to accept the gifts of grace that you offer me in every moment of my life. Open my eyes to recognize the little miracles you send my way. Open my heart to your voice, however soft it may be. Help me to trust in your divine plan; help me to place my life and all my past, present, and future cares in your hands. Even when I feel alone, please help me to hold on to my faith and to remember that you are always with me.
Amen.

RECOMMENDATIONS FOR USE

Sexual abuse wounds the whole person — mind, body, and spirit. Visible scars may be the first to fade, but we are left with wounds in our minds and hearts. These inner wounds are what this devotional seeks to address.

I hope that this devotional can be a supplement for psychotherapy or spiritual counseling. It is not meant to replace those things. However, I do understand that, due to many different circumstances, not everyone reading this feels able or ready to come forward about their experiences. While I will always encourage victims to come forward when they can (whether to the police, a therapist, a priest, or a confidant), I understand that ultimately you need to be ready. I pray for all of you reading this book, but I pray especially for those of you who feel trapped in your silence. At the very least, I hope that the Holy Spirit speaks to you through each reflection, freeing you from your chains and setting you on the path to hope and healing.

How you use this devotional is up to you. I would, however, like to explain how it is set up and make some recommendations for its use. Again, these are suggestions. Everyone is different, and every person heals differently. I urge you to find what works best for you. You may choose to read this devotional all at once or take your time and meditate on each reflection, moving on to the next as you feel ready. Personally, I recommend taking it slowly and meditatively. I encourage you to work through each reflection as you are ready, and write out your thoughts, as you find it helpful, in the space provided.

The book is divided into three parts: "Finding Grace," "Finding Healing," and "Finding Freedom." Each part contains reflections on the gifts that God wants to give us throughout our healing journey. Each gift is presented with an inspiring quotation and a reflection, followed by a brief prayer and then four sections:

Embracing Grace

This is a brief positive affirmation. Following a trauma such as sexual abuse, the brain is rewired. Understandably, our thoughts become extremely negative. Practicing positive statements frequently can help to retrain the brain to think more positively. For example, "I'm a bad person" is a negative affirmation. "I'm a good person" is a positive affirmation. Positive affirmations aren't a cure-all, but they are a powerful healing tool. I have included particular phrases after each reflection. Look in the back of the book for the "Embracing Grace" section, which lists all the affirmations throughout the book and leaves space for you to write your own positive affirmations. This is a great page to flip to when you're having a particularly difficult day and need a little boost. Positive affirmations work best when repeated frequently. I found it helpful to write down one or two on sticky notes and leave them in a prominent place (such as on the bathroom mirror).

Embracing a Grateful Heart

Studies show that people who practice gratefulness tend to think more positively and are more open to accepting happiness and joy. In this section, I encourage you to find something (however small) that you are grateful for to reflect on each day — a glimmer of God's grace, if you will. Prompts are provided to help get the wheels turning. There is also an "Embracing a Grateful Heart" section at the back of the book, where you can write all the things you are grateful for. Again, this is a good page to flip to, especially on days when everything seems hopeless and bleak.

A word of caution in regard to gratitude: I strongly advise you to avoid the statement "Someone has it worse than I do." That mindset can cause more harm than good. It can lead you to believe that your thoughts and feelings don't matter, and the truth is that they do matter — very much so. There is no need to feel guilty about your own circumstances.

One Small Step

Self-care is a very important part of your healing journey. Even the seemingly little decisions that you make each day in regard to your health and wellness can affect you (either positively or negatively), and taking proper care of yourself is necessary for your ongoing healing. Caring for yourself is good for you, inside and out. Why? Because you and your needs are important. If you're looking for some basic self-care techniques, look no further; that's the primary purpose of this section. These are techniques and ideas that I have found helpful over the course of my healing journey. What works for one person doesn't necessarily work for another, though. You might find a few to be particularly helpful, in which case I encourage you to make them a regular part of your routine.

Questions for Reflection

Each chapter will be followed by a few questions for you to reflect on. You will find space to write down your answers, questions, reflections, and so forth — anything you want. If writing isn't your thing and you just don't feel you can express yourself adequately through that medium, try drawing. If music is what speaks to you, write or listen to music that expresses your thoughts. Find a form of creative expression that is most meaningful to you, and apply it to each reflection.

Final Recommendation

Because this devotional also includes a journaling component, you can consider sharing it with a loved one or a confidant. Though Jesus is always with us, helping to carry our crosses, a little human encouragement goes a long way. We were made to be social beings, and I can tell you from experience that having someone to lean on — someone to help you carry your crosses — can greatly contribute to healing. Perhaps your husband or wife, your mother or father, or a friend is trying to better understand the trauma you have experienced. Perhaps you are reading this in order to better understand what a loved one or a friend has gone through. Sharing your reflections with someone else allows him or her to get a glimpse into your thoughts and emotions. Maybe you want to work through this with your therapist, pastor, parent, or friend. Perhaps you will choose to start a different journal based on the reflections in this devotional.

Whatever your choices, however you choose to use this devotional, I am proud of you for taking the steps to heal. Always be assured that Our Lord is with you every step of the way. He is waiting to offer you his gifts. I pray for each and every one of you who picks up this book, and I hope that your eyes will be opened to the glimmers of God's grace so that you may embrace these moments of hope and peace.

PART I

FINDING GRACE

Pause and Pray

Dear Lord,
*I lift my eyes, heart, and hands to you and cry out in anguish!
I come to you laden with a heavy cross. You see all and know
all. You have seen how much I have been hurt. You know the
struggles I face. I need your help, Lord. I can't carry this cross
alone.*

*Please be with me and help me to heal as I embark on
this journey. Help me to accept the pain and suffering I have
endured. Help me to have faith, to hope, to trust, and to recognize the truth. Open my eyes to your grace. Help me to accept
the gifts you offer to me with a kind and grateful heart.*

*Please guide and protect me. Help me to overcome the
storms I face, and lead me to where I am meant to go. Amen.*

ACCEPTANCE

There are certain things you need to do, and there are other things you need to allow God to do in you.

— Matthew Kelly

Dear Friend in Christ,

Today, God offers you the gift of **acceptance**.

I want you to know how brave you are. Perhaps you don't feel very brave right now, and that's okay. You have permission to be human. It's okay not to be okay. You may feel broken, but I want you to know that you are beautiful, and in time, you will come to realize just how precious you are.

Yes, you who are reading this: You are brave, and you are beautiful. You woke up today. You picked up this book. You have been through the fires of hell to get where you are today, and yet you are still standing. Know that you are not alone. Our stories may be different, but I will be with you as you start on this journey, and of course, God is with you as you walk this path. Yes, he is there in the midst of your brokenness.

For a long time, I felt alone and abandoned by my Father. The young, innocent girl who had been so betrayed by someone so trusted, by a Catholic priest, wanted desperately to run from the brokenness. I thought that hiding from it was easier than facing it. Every time I was assaulted, I left the rectory where I was working as a weekend secretary, full of shame, confusion, and doubt. I felt drained and weak, emotionally, spiritually, and physically. I came to dread the dawn of each morning, because facing yet another day of keeping up the charade of being a normal teenage girl was just too exhausting. The silence was slowly eating away at me and destroying my spirit.

Our minds defend themselves with denial to allow us to keep functioning on a daily basis, and denial allowed me to go about my day in an apparently fairly normal manner. Living with such a big secret as sexual abuse makes it impossible for our brains to process too many emotions at once. Sadness seemed to be the only emotion I could experience. I had no visible physical wounds, and those close to me could see only that I was slowly becoming more withdrawn, my grades were suffering, the things in which I usually found so much joy became less enjoyable, and I seemed to be under a constant dark cloud. The interior wounds were far worse; even after I quit my job and the abuse mostly stopped, the wounds were there, festering in the painful silence.

I am sure that you, too, have a dark place in your mind that houses your feelings of betrayal, disgust, unworthiness, anger, and that utter lack of control over your circumstances. A recurring nightmare caused me to wake up many a night, making me feel afraid and vulnerable; even as I went about my normal day, that nightmare haunted me. I felt as though I were living in constant terror, and after a while I realized that I could not get out of that dark pit of my dreams alone.

In desperation, I turned to Jesus. I needed someone greater than me, but I felt so unworthy to ask him for help. I began to pray with great trepidation. Sure, I knew how to pray, and I regularly rattled off the Rosary, meal blessings, and Mass responses. I lived in a home where our Catholic faith was central to our everyday lives; but during those months of abuse, I felt abandoned by my heavenly Father.

One day, I looked at a painting of Jesus praying in the Garden of Gethsemane. The words from the Gospel came to mind, "My Father, if it be possible, let this chalice pass from me; nevertheless, not as I will, but as you will" (Mt 26:39). I remember feeling as though my eyes had been opened for the first time. Not only did Jesus experience tremendous fear, but he also accepted that, alone, he could not face what was to come. He reached out to his Father for help, and in doing so, he was able to accept his Passion.

Think about that for a moment: Jesus, the Son of God, asked for help. He knew he wasn't alone. Neither are you alone in your torment. Our Lord hears you, he sees you, he understands your pain. He doesn't want any of us to suffer! Sadly, sin is a part of this world, and we sometimes suffer because of the sins of others. God doesn't cause our woundedness, but when we are wounded, God wills that we turn our pain over to him. He wants so much for us to experience his unconditional grace and love.

I, too, wasn't alone, despite what my tormented mind was telling me. Jesus had been with me all along, especially in the midst of my suffering. My pain was joined to his pain on the cross. He bore my cross with me. All I needed to do was say yes to the precious gifts he offered. Simon of Cyrene was forced to help Jesus carry his cross, but Jesus willingly helps us bear ours.

You are not alone. No one understands what you are going through more than Jesus. He knows your fear, and he wants to be with you as you seek to accept your cross. Acceptance of your experiences is about acknowledging things that have been out of your control. Acceptance of past hurts, and the grief you feel as a result, leads to healing. Acceptance does not mean forgetting about the past, but rather, allowing God to take control of your pain and to give you the gifts and graces you need to work through it. Your journey to freedom begins with acceptance. You are worth more than anything that anyone has done to you.

You are brave because you are willing to accept and face the pain that binds you. You are brave because you have a desire to heal. You desire hope; you desire to be renewed in your faith; you want to close those deep wounds. Just as the glory of the Resurrection came from the suffering and death of Our Lord, so will you one day feel the glory of new life as you unite the pain of your past to Christ.

You are not alone, dear one. Today, bring your pain to the One who is greater than death itself. Share your darkest memories with him. He already knows them, but you need to speak them so that you can release them and begin to heal. Invite him into the darkness and ask him to deliver you from the pain that holds you captive. Invite him into your heart, and ask him to be with you as you begin your healing journey. If you are ready and able and haven't done so already, I encourage you to find at least one person you can share your burden with, someone who can help bear your cross, whether a loved one, a friend, or a counselor.

Wherever you are at this moment on your path, ask Our Lord to meet you there. His hand is outstretched. He patiently waits for you to grasp it. Renowned author and stress-management counselor Loretta LaRoche, reminds us, "There's so much grace in acceptance. It's not an easy concept, but if you embrace it, you'll find more peace than you ever imagined."

Prayer
Dear Father, please guide me on my healing journey. Help me to accept what has been and what is, and to have faith in what is to come.

Embracing Grace
I am worthy of receiving God's great gifts.

Embracing a Grateful Heart
What is something that makes you smile?

Seeing the soft side of humanity, those moments when people don't think anyone is watching, and so they laugh to themselves about something entirely in their minds, their own little worlds.

One Small Step: Get Moving

and for a moment, they share with us what is going on in

Going through any kind of trauma is not only emotionally and spiritually taxing but physically taxing as well. If you aren't already regularly physically active, find a few minutes to go for a brisk walk, even if you're just marching in place in the house for a few minutes. Or find an at-home walking workout on YouTube. My favorite trainer is Leslie Sansone. Her walks are gentle, and her personality is infectious. There are lots of great free videos to choose from.

Pay close attention to how you feel before you start moving versus after you finish. Move for as little or as long as your schedule and body allow. Even five or ten minutes is better than nothing. Physical exercise boosts your energy levels and releases good, happy hormones. For the next few days, try to get in a few minutes of movement whenever you can, and see how you feel. Your mind, body, and spirit are all connected; when one suffers, they all suffer. When you feel good physically, you'll feel better mentally and emotionally, and you'll be ready to tackle each day with more energy and vigor.

Questions for Personal Reflection

What experiences do you feel ready to face and accept?

I don't know if it ready because I don't know what it means to accept something. But I know that what I can now recognize is that there ~~was going~~ was a long process of desensitization and manipulation being done to me for the sake of an older man's pleasure

How can you make God a part of your healing?

For him to become a part of my healing he would have to become a part of my life first

If you are ready and haven't done so already, is there someone (a loved one, a friend, or a counselor) you trust enough to break your silence to?

Although I can't quite explain why, I feel more comfortable talking to strangers about it, probably because they don't know my ~~chara~~ ~~character~~ so they might actually believe me

FAITH

Faith is the assurance of things hoped for, the conviction of things not seen.

— Hebrews 11:1

Dear Friend in Christ,

Today, God offers you the gift of **faith**.

I know the feeling — the feeling that God has somehow betrayed and abandoned you. Life goes on around you, yet you are left standing alone in a deep pit of self-loathing, shame, and fear. Your heart probably feels as if it has been ripped out, and you're wondering if you will ever feel whole again. You may feel completely weak in yourself and even in your faith. I understand. I've been there too.

I can tell you for certain that everything you are feeling right now — the ups and downs, the confusion, the pain, the complete turmoil and chaos — is normal. I know it's scary and intimidating to face your pain. It's tough to dig down into the deepest recesses of our hearts and allow ourselves to be vulnerable.

Can I share some good news with you? You are not alone. There is someone who has felt your pain: blow for blow, torment for torment, scar for scar. That person is Jesus. And he ever so gently offers you the tremendous gift of faith.

The sad reality is that there is evil in our world. We all suffer in one way or another due to the effects of original sin. Even Our Lord and Savior, who was born free from original sin, embraced our fallen state and underwent a greater suffering than any of us can begin to imagine. Though I may never truly understand the hows and whys of suffering, I do know that faith is a big part of getting through it. Faith isn't always something we feel or see. We don't always have proof of what we believe. Yet having faith means trusting in God's love even when we don't immediately understand why we are suffering, where we are headed, or what God's plan may be. In the words of Mother Angelica, "Faith assures the soul that God is always present and cannot absent himself from it unless it rejects him." Whatever his plan, we can be assured that he will make good come out of the bad, for "we know that in everything God works for good with those who love him, who are called according to his purpose" (Rom 8:28).

In Mother Angelica's book *Answers, Not Promises*, she says: "God never said life was going to be one smooth sail. By the example of his Son, our Savior, he showed us that we as Christians were almost guaranteed a rough time. He never said it would be fair or easy. But he did say that in his House were many mansions and that one day we would be able to see the reasons and the whys for every offense and suffering." Yes, some sort of good will come out of your suffering, and one day you will understand the whys and hows. Faith will carry you through.

Without faith, I would have given up. During my journey, I was able to receive the gift of faith only after I accepted the reality of the situation at hand. In the midst of bearing my cross, there came a time when holding on to faith became a decision. I had to choose between abandoning faith or turning to the Lord despite my doubt.

I was raised in a devout Catholic home, so faith in God had been ingrained in me from birth. It came naturally to me. I was confused when my belief in an all-loving, all-powerful God began to waver. After all, what kind of God would allow something like this happen? Why didn't he make it stop? The feelings of abandonment caused me tremendous agony. As my rapist abused and humiliated me week after week, I cried out louder and louder from within my heart, "Where are you, Lord? Help me!" A fog came over me during the attacks. I later learned that this is called dissociation, a function of the brain that helps to protect us from trauma. I felt numb and paralyzed. Praying began to feel foolish.

In my dark pit of despair, week after week, night after night, the nightmare taunted me: "Where is your Lord? See? He's not coming. You're all alone. You'll always be alone. Your Almighty God has abandoned you. Why would he love you anyway? You're not worth it. You're not worth anything."

Without faith, bitterness overwhelmed my soul. As I lost faith, I lost hope. What was I living for — to be at the mercy of this man over and over again? The words of Saint Thérèse, the Little Flower, in her autobiography, *Story of a Soul*, describing her dark night of the soul, seemed to be my own:

> When I want to rest my heart fatigued by the darkness that surrounds it by the memory of the luminous country after which I aspire, my torment redoubles; it seems to me that the darkness, borrowing the voice of sinners, says mockingly to me: "You are dreaming about the light, about a fatherland embalmed in the sweetest perfumes; you are dreaming about the eternal possession of the Creator of all these marvels; you believe that one day you will walk out of this fog that surrounds you! Advance, advance; rejoice in death which will give you not what you hope for but a night still more profound, the night of nothingness."

Reading of Thérèse's despair reassured me. Even this holy soul suffered. Even she experienced darkness and doubt. Yet, she persevered. She kept going. She held on all the more fiercely to her belief in God.

Something deep within my heart burned faintly — a light, although weak, urged me forward, and it was as though a loving, gentle voice within my heart urged, "Don't give up, dear one. Have faith." I knew there had to be something more. After all, didn't Saint Thérèse find her way out of the darkness? This assurance ultimately led me forward. I had to believe that I could get out. I had to believe that there was a God greater than anything I was going through. The decision lay before me: leave my faith behind and, as a result, lose all hope; or have faith that I would be healed and led to greater hope. I didn't know what would come, but I knew that I had to take a leap toward faith.

Over time, I discovered that faith allows me to see the good that comes out of the bad. You may be thinking, "What good could possibly come out of suffering?" The answer to that question is rarely immediate. The wonderful gift of hindsight allows us to look back on our experiences and to recognize the light that God has brought out of our darkness. My experiences have made me more patient, helped me to be more grateful and empathetic to those around me, and molded me into a much stronger person than I ever realized I could be.

We are all God's children, and we are all one in the Body of Christ. Without our even realizing it, one person's suffering affects us all. At the same time, we all have the power to use our suffering to do good and to accomplish great things, reaching out to our brothers and sisters who may be hurting. I'm not suggesting that you ever have to come forward publicly about your sexual abuse. Not everyone feels called to that, and that's okay! However, survivors do carry an extraordinary level of empathy as a result of their experiences, and you never know how your own suffering may be able to serve another (whether or not they ever know that you, too, are a survivor).

Rest assured, having faith doesn't mean that you will never have questions or doubts. It does mean that you have a place to take them. Faith means trusting in God's great grace. In my experience, having faith requires us to let go. So often, we want proof of what's going to happen. We want to be sure before we step out onto the path that lies before us. There's a reason the expression goes "take a leap of faith." The other expression I hear a lot is "faith over fear." Isn't that what Our Lord chose the night before he died? He sweat drops of blood and prayed, "My Father, if it is possible, let this chalice pass from me; nevertheless, not as I will, but as you will" (Mt 26:39). What did Jesus do? He went through with his mission; he suffered and died for me and for you and for every human being who has ever come into existence. How was he able to get past the incredible fear he experienced? He chose faith over fear. He took a leap of faith in his Father's plan. Yes, he was still afraid. But he had faith that good would come out of the injustice and evil done to him. What comes after the pain, agony, and sadness of Good Friday? The glory of the Resurrection!

Sometimes my faith feels incredibly strong, and a light burns strong and bright in my heart. Other times, such as in the midst of suffering, the light is feebly burning. It's a lot easier to believe when our hearts are bathed in sunshine, isn't it? In the darkness, holding on to faith seems a lot more difficult. That, however, is true faith — believing even when we don't feel it. Our faith in Christ reminds us that there is something better to come, even if we don't know what that is or when or where it will happen.

Now, to be clear, choosing faith isn't always easy. I have to work at my faith every single day. I'm weak. I'm only human. I get scared. I experience doubts and frustration. Yet I have come to realize that even when the darkness is enveloping me and I feel trapped, I am not alone. It is in suffering that Our Lord is closest to us. He never leaves our sides. Because of faith, through his grace, I was able to break my silence. Because of faith, I was able to find hope in healing. Faith helped to give me strength enough to face my rapist at a trial. Faith helped me to persevere even in moments of great despair, when life didn't seem worth living. Faith helped me to recognize God's love and grace.

Dear friend, God wants you to share your experiences with him. He wants you to be completely honest with him, no matter how painful your suffering. He can take it. Evil has been done to you, and God desires to bring good from it. If I've learned one thing over the course of my life, it's this: Only God can restore what is broken. With faith, there is hope. Healing, especially of the emotional and spiritual kind caused by abuse, doesn't happen in an instant, but faith (and time) will move you forward.

Today, accept God's great gift of faith. Jesus tells us that our faith can move mountains (see Mt 17:20), so just imagine what a little faith can do to help you in your healing.

Prayer
Dear Jesus, please guide me on my healing journey. During times when I am confused or don't know where I'm going, keep the light of faith burning within my heart.

Embracing Grace
I have faith that good will come out of my experiences. I can heal.

Embracing a Grateful Heart
What is something in nature that you are grateful for?

the sun's warmth and weed (jw)

One Small Step: Meet the Saints
In addition to Jesus and Mary, the only two humans of perfect faith, I find much inspiration in the lives of the saints. They are real-life people who were far from perfect and yet possessed profound and deep faith, even if they did not always feel it. While some saints were blessed with great visions and consolations from Our Lord, Mother Mary, and other saints and angels, many others suffered throughout

their lives with few consolations. Their faith was simple yet profound. Their spiritual dryness only led them to love God all the more. Saint Thérèse of Lisieux, Saint Padre Pio, Venerable Fulton Sheen, and Saint Teresa of Calcutta are some of my personal favorites. And although she has yet to be declared a saint, Mother Angelica has also made a big impact on me. I have done a lot of reading over the course of my healing journey, and sometimes I have found it refreshing to pick up the story of a saint. We can learn so much from how they dealt with the adversities they faced over the course of their lives. The saints always reassure me as I strive for holiness that, while I may not reach perfection, there is always hope. Try taking a few minutes to look up a saint or two (or more) online or at the library. If you find someone you really feel you can relate to, consider asking that saint to accompany you on your path to healing. The more, the merrier! Some saints who suffered abuse during their lives were Agnes, Maria Goretti, Agatha, Dymphna, Monica, and Rita of Cascia.

Questions for Personal Reflection

What does faith mean to you?

_____

_____

_____

_____

_____

_____

How can you apply your faith to the circumstances you have faced?

_____

_____

_____

_____

_____

_____

How do you think faith can help you?

_____

_____

_____

_____

_____

HOPE

I plead with you — never, ever give up hope. Never doubt, never tire, and never become discouraged. Be not afraid.

— Pope Saint John Paul II

Dear Friend in Christ,

Today, God offers you the gift of **hope**.

One of my main reasons for writing this devotional was to offer you hope. I want to reassure you, dear one, that you can heal. There is light at the end of the tunnel. With Jesus by your side, there is always hope. The fact that you are willing to pick up this book tells me that you have confidence that you can continue to move forward.

We throw the word "hope" around so often. We hope for good weather. We hope for a good grade on that big test. We hope that someone feels better. The true meaning of "hope" seems to get lost, and the word becomes no more than an empty wish for something. Hope is so much more than a wish. It is the realization that we can look to the future with confidence, knowing that Our Lord is with us. There was, I realized, so much hope to be found even in the midst of suffering.

Just as with faith, looking to the future with optimism does not mean that you will never experience fear. After all, the future, with all its uncertainty, can be a scary thing, can't it? But Jesus suffered for us with more love than we could ever imagine, in order to bring us hope. Without hope, there is no reason to get out of bed every single day. No matter how small, a ray of hope can help to urge us forward in our everyday lives.

Hope sure doesn't come easy when you have experienced trauma. The demon of doubt envelops us, convincing us, first, that there is no way out of the abuse, then persuading us to remain silent about the abuse, and later attempting to assure us that we will never heal. For a long time, I felt so accustomed to sad, negative feelings that hope seemed like a foreign concept. I would suppress any feelings of optimism because they didn't feel normal. When your brain has been rewired due to trauma and is stuck in survival mode, feeling hopeful can be very difficult.

In a homily during his 2008 visit to Washington, D.C., Pope Benedict XVI said, "One who has hope lives differently." Later that day, during a private meeting with the Holy Father, one of the last things he said to me was, "There is always hope." His words have resonated in my heart ever since. I have seen this reality in my life and in the lives of so many people around me who have experienced suffering. The more I lost my faith, the more the darkness of bitterness and despair seeped into my heart. Just as I had to choose to have faith, I also had to choose to hold on to hope. Not feeling any emotion attached to a particular virtue doesn't mean that you do not possess the gift of it. Just as my faith wasn't restored overnight, neither did I wake up one morning having complete confidence in my future. It was a gradual process once I realized that there had to be something better. While I had the support of my loved ones and the help of a reputable Christian therapist, what really gave me hope was the cross.

The greatest symbol of hope is the cross. Because of the cross, suffering, pain, and even death are not meaningless. Think about that for a moment. Christ died for you, for me, and for every single human being who has ever come into existence, in order to bring us hope. He was willing to go through the indescribable pain and humiliation of death on the cross. Holy Week is probably my favorite week in the Church calendar, and I think it's because I can relate (albeit only a little) to the pain, fear, and betrayal Jesus experienced. Reading about his agony in the garden gives me goosebumps. The betrayal by one of his followers makes me think of the betrayal by my rapist, a man I trusted. Jesus felt fear, and yet he put his cup of suffering into God the Father's hands with complete trust and hope that everything would turn out all right. Good Friday was not the end. It was just the beginning. Consider for a moment what the pain, suffering, and sadness of that day led to. Everything led to the Resurrection on Easter Sunday. Christ's suffering was not for nothing. His sacrifice caused the gates of heaven to open for us so that one day we may share in the glory of eternal life.

Just as the sadness, pain, and suffering of Good Friday is always followed by the Resurrection, so does hope always follow adversity. Dawn always follows night. Faith in God brings hope for the future. I suffer from anxiety, and I worry a lot — just ask my husband. However, putting myself at the foot of the cross reminds me to look to Jesus' example. He had faith. He never gave up hope. Is it easy? Not always. Is it worth it? You bet!

Occasionally, even after all these years, I fall into the pit of despair and anxiety, but I have learned to turn toward my Lord. When I do, it's as if a dark cloud lifts away to reveal glimmers of sunshine. Remember, we have faith that something good came out of Good Friday, and so we look forward to Easter Sunday with hope.

"Be not afraid" to ask God for the gift of hope. Whenever you feel anxious, overwhelmed, or triggered, remember that God has something beautiful and good planned for you. Take a moment or two to gaze upon the crucifix and be reminded that the Resurrection comes after Good Friday. Allow hope to be a part of your healing action plan. Taking action to heal helps to fill you with hope. "Life is messy, but nobody can take your hope from you," says Matthew Kelly. I assure you, Our Lord's hope will shine through your sorrow. There are better things to come. You can have certainty of his great grace. With Jesus by your side, one day you will look back on your life and say, "How did I get through something so horrible?" Hope is sure to be one of the answers.

Prayer
Dear Jesus, please guide me on my healing journey. Help me to recognize that you are my hope. Fill me with the light of hope, and help my fears to decrease.

Embracing Grace
I have hope in the future.

Embracing a Grateful Heart
What is something you use every single day that helps to simplify your life?

_____

_____

_____

_____

One Small Step: Finding Your Support System
When I look back and reflect on my healing journey, I realize that there were many people who came into my life in one way or another who gave me hope. Some of these people were in my life for a short time, others for a long time. I had my own list of people who were my support: my parents, my therapist, a very holy priest whom I had known my whole life, my brothers, and a close friend. I encourage you to find your support system. If you can, find even one or two people who will pray with you, encourage you, and support you in whatever way you need it.

Questions for Personal Reflection

How can hope help you to move forward in your healing?

_____

_____

_____

_____

_____

_____

What are some things that you are afraid of?

_____

_____

_____

_____

_____

How can hope help you through those fears?

_____

_____

_____

_____

_____

TRUST

Do not fear anything. I am with you. These matters are in My hands and I will bring them to fruition according to My mercy, for nothing can oppose My will.

— Our Lord to Saint Maria Faustina Kowalska,
Divine Mercy in My Soul

Dear Friend in Christ,

Today, God offers you the gift of **trust**.

You've been fighting a battle, a battle that has probably, at times, felt unwinnable. Yet here you are. You're still standing. You've escaped with many battle wounds. If you're at the beginning of your journey, you may be finding it hard to believe that you will heal. I've gone through my share of doubts too. Physical bruises and pain sometimes fade, although sometimes they may cause lasting pain. Invisible wounds run deep and pierce your very soul. Whatever your pain, I want you to know that it is valid and it matters.

You were hurt in a way that no one should ever be hurt. Your sadness is real. Your grief is real. Your anger is real. Your anxiety is real. Your wounds (physical, emotional, and spiritual) are real. The horrible way you were treated was not normal or right. Everything you are feeling after the fact, however difficult, is normal. It's inevitable that your sense of trust has been damaged. You may be struggling to trust yourself, other people, God, and the healing process.

In a society where quick and easy solutions are so readily available at the touch of a button, healing of the mind, body, and spirit aren't quite so easily remedied. Regaining the ability to trust is a process, just as healing is a process. God offers you the gift of trust, that you may trust in your ability to heal and trust that he will work with you to heal you. You will get to know yourself again. Your wounds hurt, but with time, prayer, and God's grace, the memories will lessen in their intensity. The difficulties you have faced will not always be in the forefront of your thoughts.

In the beginning, your guard is up. You build walls to protect yourself. I certainly did. Yet there came a time when I needed to let my guard down enough to allow others into the fortress I had built to protect my heart. In hindsight, the walls slowly started to come down from the moment I decided to tell someone about the sexual abuse I had endured.

As an innocent child, I trusted so easily and so deeply. Out of four children, I was the only girl, and Dad was my hero. I worshiped the ground he walked on, and I trusted him implicitly. I vividly recall the time one summer when we were on vacation as a family, when he encouraged me to swim on my own out to a raft in the middle of the pond. My brothers were nervous, but I hardly hesitated. Dad had said that I'd be okay, and he promised that he'd be right by my side the whole time. Determined, I kicked my feet and paddled my arms toward my goal. The best part of reaching the raft was seeing the proud, beaming face of my dad. I had trusted him; he had believed in me; and he had held true to his promise. I had reached the raft safe and sound.

Such a beautiful and profound gift a child has — to be able to trust! Yet, sadly, so often that trust is corrupted and destroyed all too soon when we are forced to encounter the harsh realities of our imperfect world. My trust in my Father in heaven was just as strong as my trust in my earthly father, yet almost overnight, because of the sins of another human being, that trust, too, began to shatter. I was raped by a Catholic priest, so I sometimes still struggle to trust priests. The white collar is a known trigger for me. Thankfully, I've been able to work through it, but from time to time a memory might pop up, and suddenly that white collar is the last thing I want to look at. Trusting men of my rapist's nationality took time. I also found his native language to be extremely triggering. Our brains form certain ideas about things based on our experiences. In other words, our brain tries to warn us when it senses potential signs of danger based on its experiences so that we can create a plan of action to protect and defend ourselves. I had to work through those triggers and gain back some of the trust I had lost, and that took time. (For more about triggers and how they work, see page 103.)

Perhaps you are struggling to trust people of a certain sex; perhaps you were hurt by someone in a position of authority; or maybe it's a certain type of person you are finding it hard to trust (such as a person of a particular skin color or nationality, or someone working a particular job). No matter what your situation, no matter who your abuser was, when you have experienced such a betrayal, trust is not immediately or easily restored.

Trust needs to be built. Trust can be proven by being earned. Over time, you gather evidence that tells you whether you can or can't trust a person. Trust in human beings is not infallible. Yet, if we wish to accept help from others on our healing journey, we desperately need the gift of trust.

You may have heard this before, but asking for help is not a weakness — it's a strength. To admit, "I can't do this alone" takes strength. What steps you take are always your choice, and there are many factors involved in each person's life, but you need trust to be able to bring a psychotherapist, a counselor, or a police officer into your trauma and healing.

After my initial act of trust, I had to trust the process of healing. Even on days when I felt as if I had gone ten steps backward, I had to trust that things would get better. If I didn't trust, I would have lost all hope and probably would have been too frustrated and depressed to continue on.

Perhaps you are struggling to trust even yourself. I felt as if I was a bad judge of character because my rapist had coerced me into believing that he was my friend who really cared for my well-being. For a long time, I was afraid to trust myself and my own intuition. However, trying to heal on my own was just too painful and too heavy a cross. Yes, I knew God was with me, but I also craved earthly, human comfort. Slowly, I began to allow into my healing certain people who could assist me on my journey. I opened my heart to my therapist, to my parents and family, and to a few very trusted individuals.

The good news is that you don't have to face the torrent of feelings alone. You can trust God to heal your wounds. And, yes, I do understand that your trust in God may have suffered as well. You have likely suffered the deluge of questions: "Why didn't you stop it? Where were you?" If you are struggling to trust Our Lord, know that he understands. He wants to help. If you haven't already, is there any way you can open the door to him, so that he can fill you with his grace? He wants you to trust that he will bring something good out of your pain. He has a plan for you: "For I know the plans I have for you ... plans for welfare and not for evil, to give you a future and a hope" (Jer 29:11). God makes all things new.

Faith allowed me to stop asking why and to understand that God didn't want the abuse to happen. It happened because of human beings' ability to practice free will. It was because of one human being's selfishness and adherence to evil. My rapist was to blame, not God. That being said, it took me a long time to get to a place where I understood that truth. Sadly, human beings let one another down. We fall. We cave in to temptation, and we sin. Our sin hurts others even when we don't realize it. We are, after all, one in the Body of Christ. But even though we can't always trust our fellow humans, we shouldn't allow that distrust to affect our relationship with God. He is the one person we can trust completely all the time. God always keeps his promises. If you doubt that for a moment, just pick up the Bible and read through the Old Testament. God promised to lead the Israelites into the Promised Land (which he did). He promised to send a Savior (he did). He promised that Abraham's descendants would be as numerous as the stars (they were). These are just a few examples — time and time again, God has proven that he can be trusted.

God is such a mystery to us, and we have no idea how he's working in any given situation. We are merely human, and he is divine; therefore, we can't fathom or understand how he works or why. First, we need faith to accept that he is working, in ways we don't understand. We can rely on faith to trust that we will probably never get proof of how God is working in our lives and how he intends to use our suffering for good. As Saint Padre Pio said, "A soul who trusts in her Lord and places all her hope in him has nothing to fear."

Hold on to faith, never lose hope, and strive to trust again. Your pain can heal, and your wounds will mend with time. There are people out there who desire to offer you help, who want to support your healing. Our Lord asks that you trust in him. He will handle the rest. In the words of Saint Alphonsus Liguori, "He who trusts himself is lost. He who trusts in God can do all things."

Prayer
Jesus, help me to open myself to being helped by others. Help me to trust the process of healing, and, most of all, help me to trust in you.

Embracing Grace
Jesus, I trust in you.

Embracing a Grateful Heart
What is something you are good at doing?

_____

_____

_____

_____

One Small Step: Finding a Healthy Balance

Sometimes you just need a moment to feel grounded and reminded who you are. Finding a healthy balance between our spiritual lives, family, work, and so forth is difficult in and of itself. Add confronting a trauma to the list, and it can be easy to feel completely overwhelmed. When we are dealing with the trauma of sexual abuse, many of the activities we once found relaxing or fun understandably get tossed to the wayside. One way to practice good self-care is to consider what activities bring you joy. What fun or leisure activities do you enjoy? Perhaps there is something you used to do for fun but haven't done in a long time. Some examples might be fishing, sewing, hiking, writing, drawing, dancing, and traveling. Make a conscious effort to pick up an activity that you enjoy (or once enjoyed). Take some time to delight in being you.

Questions for Reflection

Who or what are you struggling to trust right now?

_____

_____

_____

_____

_____

_____

Is there anyone in your life you feel you can trust? Do you feel you can trust God?

_____

_____

_____

_____

_____

How can you open your mind and heart to trusting enough to accept help and support from others?

_____

_____

_____

_____

_____

TRUTH

[The devil] was a murderer from the beginning, and has nothing to do with the truth, because there is no truth in him. When he lies, he speaks according to his own nature, for he is a liar and the father of lies.

— John 8:44

Dear Friend in Christ,

Today, God offers you the gift of **truth**.

You didn't deserve what happened to you. I know this may be difficult for you to hear and accept, but it wasn't your fault. You are worth so much more than any abuse that has happened to you. You deserve to find hope, joy, and peace. You deserve healing. You deserve to be freed from the lies that have held you in chains. You deserve God's gift of truth. "If there is one thing that will give you freedom, it is truth," Matthew Kelly says.

Although the physical part of sexual abuse was difficult for me, the emotional and spiritual trauma lasted much longer and was far more painful. The priest who raped me betrayed not only me, but also a whole community of faithful, trusting parishioners. When I came forward, most people were supportive of me, but some individuals still supported him (quite publicly) and just couldn't believe that such a "nice man" could do such a thing. My rapist was a master manipulator, as are all abusers. Abusers try to cut their victims off from the rest of the world (including the victim's loved ones and friends), and one of the ways they may do this is by making efforts to be extremely likable and approachable. People believe and see what the abuser wants them to, and the truth often becomes clouded with his or her lies.

There's another master manipulator known for his evil tactics and lies of defamation: the father of lies, Satan. He uses the lies we come to believe about ourselves when we are vulnerable, and he wants us to accept those lies as truth. Abusers lie to gain trust. They lie to keep their victims quiet. They manipulate and lie until their victims are full of such shame and fear that silence seems like the best option. (See appendix II, "The Reality of Sexual Grooming.") Satan works through those men and women who seek to manipulate, shame, and abuse. He takes delight in the suffering of the innocent. He delights in the lies that torment the mind as a result of trauma. His goal is to manipulate your feelings of shame, fear, and doubt so that you will turn away from God and lose all hope. Satan doesn't want you to heal. He wants to keep you in the darkness of despair.

The brain is a very complex and mysterious organ, but we know that trauma alters the brain, rewiring it. When we experience something as traumatic as sexual abuse, our brains do whatever they need to do to protect themselves. We become sad, angry, depressed, and anxious, and it becomes difficult to concentrate on much else other than the abuse we are experiencing. The brain's one goal is to do whatever it needs to do to survive. The brain begins to reflect our experiences, and negative thinking begins to invade our thoughts. When it senses a potential threat to survival, the fight-or-flight response is activated. This provides the body with an energy burst so that it can defend itself. The devil, of course, uses this to his advantage and wants nothing more than to see us become worn down by these lies. In his book *The*

Promise: God's Purpose and Plan for When Life Hurts, Fox News contributor Jonathan Morris tells us: "In moments of particular weakness, pain, or trauma, we are more susceptible to believing non truths. Our increased sensibility in these moments gives the devil fertile ground for planting his lies deep in our souls."

What does the father of lies taunt you with? What lies hold you captive? Has he tried to convince you that you are alone or that God was never with you? Are you wrapped in the chains of shame? Does he try to tell you that you will never be free of those chains? Has he convinced you that you will never trust another human being ever again? Does he taunt you by saying that you are lying or that no one will believe you? Has he convinced you that you are to blame and that you are worthless? Does he want you to believe that you will never heal and that you will forever be trapped in silence? My dear friend, I understand the doubts, frustrations, and fears you are facing. I've believed every lie there is. My heart truly hurts to think of your pain. When your mind and heart have been so inebriated with lies that those lies have become your reality, this is a pain like no other.

When we are overcome with these lies, moving forward may seem impossible. Discovering the truth is not a simple task but, with God's help and grace, you have the power to sift through layer after layer of lies and replace those untruths with truths. No matter what your brain is telling you, you are not a failure. Sexual abuse does not define you.

We find truth only in Christ. The devil doesn't want you to believe the truth. You may be asking, "But where was God in my suffering?" Here's the truth: He was suffering with you. He was weeping with you. He was holding you. "Well, then," you may ask, "why didn't he stop it from happening?" Here's another truth: God gave each human the gift of free will. Adam and Eve chose to use their free will to turn against God, and ever since, sin has been a part of this world. Some people choose to do good, but others choose evil. If God were to prevent people from committing evil, he would be going against his gift of free will to us. We are not puppets. No one is manipulating our strings, forcing us to move this way or that. Sadly, when someone chooses evil over good, someone else suffers as a result.

Morris encourages you not to trade your "gift of freedom and self-determination for the right to live in perpetual misery ... because someone else [has] entered and taken control of [your] life." God's grace is greater than any lie and more powerful than any abuse you have faced, whether physical, sexual, emotional, spiritual, or all of the above. He offers you truth, that you may find relief and solace. He wants to help you muck out all of those lies, tricks, and empty promises. Why? Because you are his precious child. Have faith in him. Have hope. Trust in him. In him, you will find truth. *The Catechism of the Catholic Church* reminds us: "In Jesus Christ, the whole of God's truth has been made manifest. 'Full of grace and truth,' he came as the 'light of the world,' he is *the Truth*. ... To follow Jesus is to live in 'the Spirit of truth,' whom the Father sends in his name and who leads 'into all the truth'" (2466).

Prayer
Dear Father, help me to see past the lies that permeate my mind and heart. Help me to see the truth and to accept that I am your precious child.

Embracing Grace
I am a precious child of God, and I am worthy of his love and grace.

Embracing a Grateful Heart
What is a favorite quote that brings you comfort?

_____

_____

_____

_____

One Small Step: Facing the Lies
Sexual abuse creates harmful thought patterns, lies that we come to believe about ourselves (for example, it's my fault, I'm dirty, or I'm a bad person). The good news is that the brain can be changed, and

you can help your brain reorient itself to more positive, healthier behaviors and thoughts. While extensive training is more appropriately orchestrated by a professional (such as a psychotherapist), there are little exercises you can do on your own to help retrain your brain.

Here's a little exercise I found extremely helpful, and I hope you will too. Write down your list of lies. Then, for every lie you tell yourself, write a truth. To give you an idea of what I mean, I'll share with you the list of lies I used to tell myself repeatedly, followed by a list of truths.

Faith's Lies	Faith's Truths
Whatever I do isn't enough. I will never heal.	I am strong, and I am taking the steps I need to in order to heal.
The rape was my fault.	It wasn't my fault.
I should have told someone sooner.	I came forward when I was able and ready to.
My body is dirty.	My body is precious.
No one can help me.	I am learning to heal.
I am unworthy of feeling kindness and love.	I am worthy of love.
I am unworthy of experiencing joy.	I am worthy of joy.
I'm worthless.	I am worthy of God's grace.
I can't control what I feel.	My feelings are normal, and I can work through them.
I will never be safe again.	I am safe, and I am learning to trust again.

Notice that the truths are the opposites of the lies. You can use a positive affirmation to combat a lie or even find Bible passages to affirm your truths. As often as possible, I encourage you to look at your list of truths. Repeat them often. You can copy one or two of them on paper every day, record yourself reciting them and replay the recording regularly, or write the truths on a sticky note and stick it in a prominent place where you will see it often.

However you strive to retain your truths, you are helping to retrain your brain. In essence, you are taking out a bad recording and putting in a new, improved recording. With time and consistency, the bad recording can and will fade out. In his book, Morris says, "Simply replacing lies with truths (even biblical truths) can help someone establish a semblance of stability in their lives and is a necessary step toward full mind renewal." While this isn't a cure-all, it is certainly a big step and will allow you to better open yourself to God's grace, so that he can work in your life more than you ever imagined. Yes, those negative thoughts will get better. There is hope. Remember that God said, "I know the plans I have for you … plans for welfare and not for evil, to give you a future and a hope" (Jer 29:11).

Insert your name here: _____'s Lies

_____

_____

_____

_____

Insert your name here: _____'s Truths

_____

_____

_____

_____

Questions for Reflection

What are some of the negative beliefs you harbor about yourself?

_____

_____

_____

_____

_____

_____

How do you think God can help you overcome those lies and find the truth?

_____

_____

_____

_____

_____

_____

KINDNESS

Let no one ever come to you without leaving better and happier.
Be the living expression of God's kindness; kindness in your face,
kindness in your eyes, kindness in your smile.

— Saint Teresa of Calcutta

Dear Friend in Christ,

Today, God offers you the gift of **kindness**.

After sexual abuse, we are so often left feeling out of control. The memories are in the forefront of our minds — we think of little else. How can we? We've been through a traumatic ordeal, one that literally changes how we think and feel. We may be suffering from PTSD, anxiety, and depression. Memories of the trauma are cruel and painful. Facing memories in order to process and work through them is not easy. Living with trauma is like being stuck in a thick fog: We feel as though we're going around in circles but never finding a way out. When we're feeling miserable, accepting the kindness of others can be difficult. Showing kindness to others can also feel like a burden.

But listen to the truth: You are worthy! You deserve to be treated with respect and dignity. You deserve to heal. You deserve to feel
hope. You deserve God's grace. You deserve to be treated with kindness. Kindness is a gift that God gives you, but it is also a gift that is
offered by the people who care about you. And it can be a gift that you
offer to others.

I remember that, in the midst of facing my sexual abuse, I found
it hard to accept positive emotions — about myself or about others. I
had become so accustomed to feeling depressed that each day became
simply about survival. I was feeling so numbed by negative emotions
that I was almost incapable of accepting the kindness of others, even
those closest to me. My traumatized mind and aching heart couldn't
fully process when someone was trying to show me kindness, nor did
I feel worthy of receiving kindness. My sense of others' kindness was
warped by the tactics my abuser had used to groom me.

Without meaning to, I took for granted the people I loved most.
I lashed out at them. Don't we so often lash out at the people who
mean the most to us, because we feel safest and the least vulnerable
with them? It's a normal side effect of trauma, known as transference.
Our anger becomes misplaced, and instead of blaming the abuser, we
find someone closer to us — someone more immediate — to take our
anger out on. I particularly lashed out at my parents, the two people
who tried to help me the most, the two human beings in my life who
loved and supported me most. Even more, I lashed out at my Creator.
I was angry. I was bitter. I was resentful.

When my parents tried to pray with me, I resented them. I resented going to church with them. I even blamed them for the trauma I had undergone. We humans have a desire for knowledge and a
desire to know and to understand. But the suffering I had endured
was not something easily explained, especially to a fifteen-year-old.
I was confused, all over the place, and I didn't understand what I
needed. There were days when things such as school, therapy, and
even family life just seemed like one more thing. I didn't want to
think about any of those things. Hiding in my own small corner of
the universe seemed to be the best option.

In hindsight, I realize that I was blessed with a really great support system. At the time, I didn't appreciate how wonderful the people in my life were or how kind they were being. As I slowly processed the trauma, as I developed better coping skills, and as things slowly but surely got easier to contend with, I came to realize the kindness and devotion that my parents in particular were showing me. As my mind freed up a bit, I slowly came to understand that while my parents had not been sexually abused, as I had, they had been victimized in a different way. My trauma had become their trauma. Just as I was learning to cope, they were learning to cope with the reality that their daughter had been hurt so badly and that her life (and theirs) would never be the same. I knew I had to come out of myself a bit and show them more kindness. It did not come easily. I had been deeply scarred on more than one occasion by hurtful comments made by some people close to me. I was told that I was a basket case and that I brought everyone else down around me. That hurt deeply.

Truth be told, through no fault of my own, I really was a mess. However, I never intended to pass on that negativity to those around me. I was so focused on what I needed to survive my ordeal that I didn't have enough bandwidth to consider how everyone around me was doing. I had to begin showing kindness even to those individuals who didn't fully grasp what I was going through. Sadly, not everyone is supportive. I had some individuals basically say, "It happened; now move on." That is some of the worst advice anyone can give you. Moving on, just like that, is not possible. Healing takes time.

I want to reassure you that you are allowed to have bad moments. It's okay to feel helpless. Chances are, you will lash out at one time or another. When it happens, I encourage you to try to take a moment to breathe and to remind yourself where your anger should be aimed: at your abuser and at the father of lies, the devil. There are good people in the world who genuinely want to help. There are people who care and who love you. They want to help you heal. They are showing kindness. Perhaps it's a family member, a friend, a priest, someone from church, a counselor, or someone you least expect to want to help you.

To be clear, I did not trust easily after my sexual abuse. To this day, my trust needs to be gained, and that's not always a bad thing. A certain amount of caution should be used when new people and situations come into your life. I also became more aware of toxic relationships and how they affected me. Without even meaning to, I pushed people away, especially in high school, and in some cases, that wasn't necessarily a bad thing. Toxic relationships, particularly when we are vulnerable, are not worth holding on to. Some people, whether family members or friends, need to be kept at arm's length. Someone who drags you down is not someone to keep close to you. I had to be more mindful of how certain people treated me and of my reactions to them; if I found that a certain individual was causing me to become more angry and resentful, I had to take a step back.

The anger you feel is not a bad thing. Anger is a normal human emotion, and it can be righteous and just or can even move you forward. Anger, rightly placed, helps clarify a boundary. Even Jesus felt angry at those to whom anger was the appropriate reaction. Think of the story in the Gospel of Matthew, chapter 21, when Jesus drove out those who were buying and selling in the temple, his Father's house. However, showing anger and resentment toward the people trying to help will only cause your pit to get deeper.

When we are blessed with individuals who are in earnest about helping us, it is important to accept their kindness and to extend kindness to them(to the best of our ability). I remember thinking one day that perhaps Our Lord was showing me kindness through the people who were helping me. Perhaps I didn't always feel worthy, but I knew I didn't want to live a bitter life. I didn't want to be a vengeful person. How I allowed my anger to manifest itself in my life was important.

Today, allow kindness to envelop your soul. Allow yourself to be open to God's kindness and the kindness of others. In turn, strive to share that kindness with others.

Prayer
Dear Lord, help me to share your kindness with those around me, and may I always be a good reflection of your kindness.

Embracing Grace
I deserve to be treated with kindness.

Embracing a Grateful Heart
What is a positive experience in your life that brings you joy to think about?

_____

_____

_____

One Small Step: Self-Awareness
Smiling is difficult when you're going through so much inner chaos and turmoil. When I look back at pictures of myself from high school and into college, I see that I'm almost always wearing black and my shoulders are always hunched, but, most of all, I notice that I'm barely smiling, if at all. I distinctly recall telling myself, "Just smile!" I really did try. Just as I had to retrain my brain to think positively, I also had to retrain my body to reflect a more positive and confident outlook. Here's something for you to practice: Stand in front of a mirror as you would normally. How's your posture? What expression is on your face? Try standing up tall. Practice walking with your shoulders back, head held high. It will probably feel very strange at first. Also practice smiling — as a matter of fact, you can practice your positive affirmations while smiling at yourself in the mirror. Does it feel awkward and strange? Over time it will become easier, and you will become more self-aware.

Questions for Reflection

Is there someone in your life who has been particularly kind to you?

_____

_____

_____

_____

_____

How can you share kindness with those around you?

_____

_____

_____

_____

_____

How can showing kindness to others be a reflection of God's grace?

_____

_____

_____

_____

_____

How are you with receiving kindness? If it's difficult for you to show kindness but not receive it, why do you think that is? In what ways can you take those barriers down?

_____

_____

_____

_____

_____

PART II
FINDING HEALING

Pause and Pray

Dear Lord,
I feel so fragile right now. I am trying so hard to confront the pain, but it is not easy. You know better than anyone the challenges I face. Thank you for your gifts that have allowed me to get this far. Please continue to be with me and help to accept your gifts of strength, courage, wisdom, and perseverance. Help me to have patience with myself and with others. Help me to be compassionate toward myself as I strive to heal.

Open my mind and my heart to the inspiration of the Holy Spirit and the assistance that other people may offer me. When difficulties and fears arise, help me to unite myself to you on the cross. You alone know (pain for pain) what I am going through. Remind me to hope. Strengthen me; give me the courage to do what I need to do; bring me comfort; and give counsel to my family, friends, and those who are helping to guide me. Within your gentle heart, I know I can find healing. Be my strength. Allow me to feel your loving embrace as I weather this storm. Amen.

COURAGE

God's love calls us to move beyond fear. We ask God for courage to abandon ourselves unreservedly, so that we might be molded by God's grace, even as we cannot see where that path may lead us.

— Saint Ignatius of Loyola

Dear Friend in Christ,

Today, God offers you the gift of **courage**.

You are a warrior. Yes, you! You may not believe it just yet, but you are. The fact that you are here, wherever you are, in whatever time and place, means that you have courage.

Courage is a choice that we make — a choice to do something despite our fear. In *The Screwtape Letters*, C. S. Lewis notes, "Courage is not simply one of the virtues but the form of every virtue at the testing point, which means at the point of highest reality." When it comes to accepting the reality of sexual abuse, God's gift of courage helps us to face it. It's safe to say that you have felt some sort of fear surrounding your experiences. Perhaps your fear is in facing past memories, fear of getting out of a bad situation and possible repercussions from your

73

abuser, fear of coming forward, fear of not being believed, fear of being ridiculed and shamed, fear of being blamed, fear of standing up to your abuser publicly, or fear of seeking professional help.

Whatever fears you are facing right now, courage will help you to take action. As a matter of fact, you are already showing courage just based on the fact that you are picking up this book. Despite your fears, you desire (and are entitled to) healing. Getting the help you need and pursuing healing can be scary. After all, the unknown is downright frightening. Just remember that even Jesus was scared in the garden the night before he died. Rest easy, knowing that God will continue to give you courage to face your fears, and he will give you the strength to keep going.

Once I got out of the abusive situation I was in, one of the most difficult hurdles I faced was breaking my silence. About a year after quitting my job at the rectory where the abuse had taken place, my oldest brother unexpectedly passed away. The autopsy report showed a heart condition — a huge surprise to all of us, considering how healthy he had seemed. His passing shook my family to the core. Soon, my parents recognized that my grief went beyond what they knew to be normal. Of course, what they didn't realize was that I was now carrying the burden of two very serious traumas — my brother's death as well as my rape.

Going into my first session with a grief counselor, I was, quite frankly, petrified. I didn't know what therapy was like or what I was supposed to say. I sat across from a strange woman (though my parents knew and trusted her) in a strange office (although it was a pleasant, homey environment). She reassured me that this was a safe place and I could say whatever I wanted, no judgment.

I talked about my brother, but something deep within my heart urged me to tell this new person about my experience with sexual abuse. Another part of me said, "No, don't!" But I heeded the first voice and poured my heart out to her. As horrible as losing my brother was, one of the good things that came out of his death was that interior push to end my silence. Like an erupting volcano, it was all just too much to hold in. In hindsight, it was probably a good thing that the counselor's explanation of being a mandated reporter had gone completely in one ear and out the other; otherwise I might have remained silent. I was shocked when she cast no judgment upon me; she listened, wrote things down, and gently asked questions. She believed me. By the end of that session, I felt as if a huge weight had been lifted. Finally, there was someone I could talk to. Finally, there was someone I could trust.

The next step was overcoming my fear of telling my parents, the people to whom it would matter most. My therapist reassured me that my parents loved me, that they would believe me, and that they would not judge me. Their anger, she said, would be at the abuser and not at me, the abused. And so, once again, I accepted God's gift of courage. Mom and Dad responded as I had always hoped they would but never trusted enough to believe: with tears, hugs, love, concern, and unfailing support. The weight on my heart was lifted even further. The freedom I felt after breaking my silence is impossible to describe.

Sadly, I do understand that not everyone is in the same situation as I was and that not everyone is greeted with the same support. Some people from my parish, whom I had always thought highly of, supported my abuser even so far as to testify on his behalf at the trial. I needed courage to overcome my fear of facing those people in public, since running into them here and there (even at church) was unavoidable.

Facing my trauma of sexual abuse was especially scary. It's frightening to address shame and guilt, feelings caused by memories we would much rather forget all about. I didn't want to think about the nitty-gritty details of my abuse. It seemed easier to skim the surface but leave out the really deep stuff — those deep-down feelings of self-loathing that cause us to self-sabotage, often leading to unhealthy habits or addictions. I remember punishing myself for responding a certain way to the abuse, even though (in hindsight) my response was natural and involuntary. I punished myself for not running and for going back to my abuser. I felt dirty and completely powerless. As a result, I often turned to unhealthy things (such as binging and purging food) in an effort to ease my shame, guilt, and contempt, because I didn't want to, or know how to, face the underlying causes of my feelings. Sharing my story — completely, openly, and honestly — was uncomfortable, to say the least. Terrifying, really. However, scratching the surface of my experiences was not enough to begin healing. "But I'm fine," I would tell myself. No. I wasn't fine, not until every single detail, even the most awful, intimate ones, were addressed. Pushing memories and triggers aside with indifference was not enough.

Addressing sexual abuse (and all that goes with it — the emotions, memories, triggers, and everything else) is scary. We often have no idea just how much certain things are affecting us until we allow them to come to the surface and work through them. Whenever I've remembered a particularly difficult detail of my abuse, I've found it helpful to talk to God first. I figure he knows it all anyway, even without my telling him. But talking to him openly and honestly, out loud, is a starting point for me. It helps me to address the initial fear. Then, if I need to, I can work through the issue with someone from my support system.

When I talk to God, I give him every single, nitty-gritty detail. It's not until I try to verbalize my emotions and memories that I realize just how much self-hatred I've been carrying. Years may pass, and certain things that were never fully addressed may present themselves in unexpected ways — perhaps recurring illness, bodily pain or discomfort, psychological torment, or spiritual unrest. The devil will try to use these against us to bring us deeper into despair. He wants nothing more than for us to squelch our painful memories and not address them. He wants to watch our pain, misery, shame, and self-loathing grow. He delights in watching us enter into self-destructive behaviors or even harmful behaviors toward others. Addressing these things can be humbling and embarrassing.

For a lot of abuse victims, addressing the feelings that come about as a result of having been groomed by their abusers may be particularly difficult. I came to care for my abuser as a friend, spiritual adviser of sorts, and confidant. One minute I was hating him and scared of him, and the next minute I felt compassion toward him.

He had slowly and carefully led me into the feeling of a relationship, and by the time the predator struck, I was left defenseless, shocked, and feeling as if I must have asked for it. I must have "led him on somehow."

Courage helped me to face these demons as they came to the surface in therapy. Courage helped me to work through the initial anger, depression, anxiety, and internal lies that I was afraid to face while still trying to get through high school and maintain as normal an existence as possible. God gave me courage to face my rapist in court. The gift of courage allowed me to move forward into the unknown. Courage helped me to hold on to faith even when nothing seemed clear. Like so many virtues, courage is not something we automatically feel. Rather, it is a gift that strengthens over time as we make one little choice and then another — for example, the choice to get out of bed every morning even though we don't want to, or the choice to face pain head-on even though it hurts to do it. Courage is what keeps us going through the dark valley of our pain.

Not long before the trial, I vividly recall sitting before the Blessed Sacrament in church. I was feeling alone and so afraid that my whole body was shaking; I was cold, helpless, and weak. My prayer in that moment was simple: "Lord, give me courage." I felt no inner fireworks and heard no voice, but I felt a deep sense of calm. A Bible verse came to mind: "Take heart, it is I; have no fear" (Mt 14:27). I was still afraid, but so long as I kept my faith in Jesus alive and trusted in him, I knew I would not be facing my fears alone. I can never hope to be anywhere near as courageous as Jesus was, but on the cross, his suffering and death were the ultimate act of faith, trust, and courage in the face of adversity.

So, in the words of one of my favorite saints, Padre Pio, "Pray, hope, and don't worry. Worry is useless. God is merciful and will hear your prayer."

Courage does not mean the absence of fear but rather the decision to move forward despite the fear. Have faith, trust, and pray. Give your fear to God. That single act of courage will get you started, and God's strength will help you to continue on.

Prayer
Dear Holy Spirit, please give me the gift of courage to face my fears.

Embracing Grace
I have courage to face my fears.

Embracing a Grateful Heart
What gift have you been given (at any time in your life) that brought you joy?

_____

_____

_____

_____

One Small Step: Stay Hydrated
Growing up, my mom was always reminding me, "Drink plenty of water!" To this day, she reminds me to stay hydrated. Nowadays, I've become so aware of the importance of hydration that usually I'm the one giving her the reminder. She's right, though. Staying hydrated is an important part of taking care of yourself — physically and mentally. When you're dehydrated, your body suffers and makes you prone to illness. It hurts your brain too. Have you ever noticed that when you haven't been drinking enough water, your brain feels foggy? Thinking and processing become very difficult, and your mood changes. According to the Mayo Clinic, eight eight-ounce glasses of water a day is an easy-to-remember and reasonable goal, although each person's need may vary, depending on various factors. During the years when I was particularly stressed, I chose to carry a water bottle everywhere I went. To this day, I have water with me everywhere I go. It has really made a positive difference for my overall health and wellness. Today, make it a goal to drink more water if you don't drink plenty of water already.

Questions for Reflection

What are some of the things that you are fearful of on your healing journey?

_____

_____

_____

_____

_____

_____

Are there any obstacles preventing you from seeking help or from working toward healing?

_____

_____

_____

_____

_____

How can God's gift of courage help you face those fears and triumph over them?

_____

_____

_____

_____

_____

STRENGTH

God is our refuge and strength,
*   a very present help in trouble.*
Therefore we will not fear though the earth should change,
*   though the mountains shake in the heart of the sea;*
though its waters roar and foam,
*   though the mountains tremble with its tumult.*

                                                    — Psalm 46:1–3

Dear Friend in Christ,

Today, God offers you the gift of **strength**.

I don't need to tell you that surviving sexual abuse is no easy task. You've probably already realized that there are good days, when you feel as though you can see the warm, bright sun shining in a perfectly blue sky, and days when you feel as though the rain and clouds are casting a gloomy shadow over the world. Those good days are examples of glimmers of God's grace — reminders that a time will come when the days full of sunshine will outweigh the gloomy days. They encourage us to keep going and not to give up. Gloomier days can leave you feeling physically, emotionally, and spiritually exhausted. You may even wonder if continuing on this healing journey is really worth it. You may ask, "Wouldn't it be easier to just forget about my past? It'll go away, right?"

This is a lot to contend with. No matter what stage of life you are at, you've probably got a lot on your plate. Memories take over at times and can be at the forefront of your thoughts all the day through. Perhaps you are in school, have a family, are working a job, or are tending to the needs of others in some way. Wherever you are in life, whatever you are doing, trying to address your experiences with sexual abuse is a huge stressor. You have may realized already that it's not going away, no matter how much you want (or try) to suppress it. Sexual abuse is not something you can just move on from. I've heard it from people before: "Just move on. Don't worry about it. The past is the past." Here's the thing: The memories and the pain will always be there and will fester if you don't address them as they come to the surface. Everything needs to be aired so you can move on with your life in the fullest way possible. God is giving you the tools — the gifts — you need so that, with him, you can accomplish this.

While true, complete happiness is found only in heaven, brighter days are ahead in your life. Despite the difficult times, it is possible to feel joy and peace and love again by allowing God to enter into your suffering. As Saint Josemaría Escrivá says, "He did not say you would not be troubled, you would not be tempted, you would not be distressed, but he did say you would not be overcome."

I want to hold you by the hand, look you square in the eye, and reassure you: It does get better. God has offered you the gift of courage so that you may face what you fear. Now he offers you the gift of strength so that you can remain determined to stay on the healing path. He wills that you experience far more than a life of silence, pain, and fear.

We hear so often about our society's interpretation of strength. We are overwhelmingly obsessed with men and women who are tenacious and relentless superheroes doing things that are out of this world. However, when you stop and think about it, so often those who we think are the weakest among us have the strongest faith. To have strength does not mean that you are doing it all on your own or performing superhuman feats. True strength lies in one's ability to grasp onto God's unfailing grace, doing what you can as best as you can and asking others for help when you need it.

There is no shame in relying on others or admitting you can't do it all. Did not God create us to be social beings? Are we not all one in the Body of Christ? Look at the simple, humble lives of the saints to get a glimpse of true strength. Saints such as Thérèse of Lisieux, Mother Teresa, Padre Pio, and Francis of Assisi (to name a few) showed incredible strength in how they lived their lives. Despite their fears, despite the fact that they may have been seen as small and weak, they had strength through Christ that allowed them to persevere even in the midst of tremendous suffering and, at times, ridicule.

Once I worked past the various fears that I was faced with — coming forward, facing my rapist in court, testifying, and so forth — strength took over and urged me onward. Strength allowed me to get through all of the gloomy days, to admit when I was feeling weak, to go when I was able to go and stop when I needed to stop. Believe it or not, it takes strength to admit you need help, to admit you can't do it all alone, to admit you're having a rotten moment or a rotten day.

You, too, are strong, even though you may not always feel it. Someone is driving you forward; something is urging you on. That someone is God. That something is his grace. It's no accident that you are reading a book like this one. You are searching for healing, for answers, for reassurance — and God has given you the courage and strength to get where you are today. Never doubt that for a moment.

Physical strength can also be very much a factor in the healing process. Trauma leaves us feeling completely worn out and exhausted. Because of the power of the mind-body-spirit connection, our negative experiences affect our bodies too. Treating your body with the dignity, respect, and care it deserves can make a big impact on your healing.

We have to begin by recognizing our physical bodies as gifts in and of themselves. The physical scars of abuse tend to fade first, but the emotional and spiritual scars tend to hang on, and those scars can create physical discord in their turn. I was never a really physically active person until high school, when, out of desperation and in an effort to try something to help me feel better, I started exercising. Nothing fancy, just walking at first. Over time, I noticed that the physical strength I had gained as a result of exercise improved my emotional strength. I started to see my body as a gift, as part of the key to healing and to a brighter future.

Today, ask Our Lord for strength — physical, emotional, and spiritual. The gift of strength will help you to see beyond the lies of the evil one. Facing reality takes strength. Working to heal takes strength. Being strong doesn't mean that you never doubt or that you never feel as if you're failing. All these years after I was raped, I still don't always feel strong. I need Our Lord, who is my "refuge and strength" (Ps 46:1).

You survived the abuse. You will survive the healing journey as well. Always remember that true strength lies in the ability to place your burdens at the feet of God. Even when you don't feel strong, his power is "made perfect in weakness" (2 Cor 12:9). Mother Angelica explains: "Jesus knew that once he, the Son of the Father, was stretched out upon the Cross, all men of faith would obtain the strength to endure the sufferings the Father permitted in their lives. ... Pain is Jesus suffering in us, but we are to look to him for strength and courage. We are to learn this ability to shoulder our cross by gazing at him and being gentle and humble in heart."

It's humbling to admit, but I've never been strong enough, nor will I ever be strong enough, to handle adversity all on my own. Healing takes an incredible amount of trust, courage, and strength. Suffering will make you stronger if you allow it to — if you take the appropriate steps, take a healthy approach to healing, and allow

God to be your strength. You don't need to be strong on your own. God has carried you this far. He will give you strength to keep going. He is your refuge and your strength.

Prayer
God, please be my strength.

Embracing Grace
I can do all things in [Christ] who strengthens me. (Phil 4:13)

Embracing a Grateful Heart
Who is a person (from your past or present) whom you are grateful for?

_____

_____

_____

_____

One Small Step: Getting Enough Rest
Your brain has been on overload. As a result, your body is tired too. Your brain and your body need to rest. Try to get enough sleep at night (the recommendation is seven to eight hours every night for an adult). Take a power nap in the middle of the day if you need to. I know that nighttime can be difficult, and sometimes the fear of nightmares can keep you awake, so be aware of your nighttime routine. Intentionally spend time doing something calming, such as taking a bath, reading a favorite book, or praying. Praying a Rosary often helps me when I have a lot on my mind. Sometimes, when all else fails, I grab a rosary and just say the Hail Mary over and over again.

As with any self-care technique, adequate sleep is not a cure-all, but having a rested mind and body certainly makes a difference, especially on your mood and your ability to face each day.

Questions for Reflection

What steps can you take to let go of your fears and allow God to be your strength?

_____

_____

_____

_____

_____

_____

How can your experiences make you a stronger person?

_____

_____

_____

_____

_____

WISDOM

No great wisdom can be reached without sacrifice.

— C. S. Lewis, *The Magician's Nephew*

Dear Friend in Christ,

Today, God offers you the gift of **wisdom**.

You've shown great courage and strength. It takes courage and strength to face your fears. Take a moment to acknowledge that. When life throws us unexpected curve balls, we're often left standing behind the plate in confusion, wondering what just happened and what's going to happen next. Fear, doubt, and anxiety take over. So what are we to do? We can either fall into despair, or we can trust in God and allow our experiences to make us wiser.

I've had many good examples of patience in my life, and Babcia (Polish grandmother) was one of them. Her life had not been an easy one, and I often watched and marveled at her as she went about her everyday chores with determination and patience. Over the course of her life, she had developed a knack for finding the good in everything around her. She accepted some things the way they were but also fought to change the things that she could. Babcia was a simple woman and yet a wise one. Perhaps she wasn't extraordinarily book smart, and perhaps she was naive about many things, but there was a strength and wisdom about her that came from the many lessons she had learned over the course of her life — suffering that she chose to allow her to move closer to Christ, not further away.

Wisdom helps us accomplish that which seems impossible. Healing from sexual abuse may seem like a far-reaching goal right now. But wisdom allows you to sift through all the information you have about your situation and determine what is true. It allows you to determine the best solutions. With wisdom, we can recognize when to close one door and open another. "Don't let what you cannot do interfere with what you can do," Matthew Kelly emphasizes. Wisdom allows you to look back in hindsight and better understand how and why your life has unfolded the way it has.

One of the wisest modern-day individuals, I believe, was Mother Angelica. She truly understood suffering and wisdom; she said, "Often we pray to the Father when we want him to change something in our lives. But God's permitting will sees beyond the present moment to the bounds of eternity. If things don't change, it is because he understands, far more than we ever will, the necessity of our living through that situation." We don't understand why, but God in his wisdom knows why, how, and when.

I know it may seem hard to believe, but you can experience personal growth in suffering. At first glance, trauma seems impossible to deal with and to overcome. However, when we accept our trauma and slowly realize that we can overcome it, the impossible becomes possible and we experience tremendous growth. No, suffering alone does not make us wiser. In and of itself, suffering leaves us weak and shattered. When we ignore it, we become weaker, and everything seems even bleaker and impossible. But when we open the door to allow God to enter into our suffering, we are essentially opening the door to the invaluable opportunity for personal growth.

I am not suggesting that you will never have a miserable day again. I do assure you, from my experience, that you will have more good days than bad. I promise that, by accepting God's gift of wisdom, you are opening your heart and mind to gaining insight about yourself, about others, and about the world around you. This insight can be valuable to you, and it can be extremely valuable to others, to your brothers and sisters in Christ.

You may not realize it, but your story is a story of hope. You have gained a very unique perspective about suffering, and it enables you to better empathize with what others might be going through. To be clear, your story is your own, and whether you share it with others is your choice. Not everyone is called to share parts of their lives openly, so just know that whatever you feel called to do is your choice. You have had a lot taken from you, but this is something you should be in control of.

All these years after my trauma, I am not a psychological expert on sexual abuse — I can't rattle off statistics and theories to you. But I can sure explain the grief process that accompanies sexual abuse. I can empathize with you and with anyone who has experienced trauma. I've lost a lot, but I've also gained powerful life lessons that I still apply to my life each and every day — lessons of faith, strength, courage, patience, perseverance, and so forth. Wisdom allows me to understand certain elements of the human existence that I could never truly understand just by reading a book.

God's wisdom far surpasses my own. I find that it is necessary to trust in his wisdom and to let go when I need to. Sometimes I try to drive when I really need to be allowing God to drive. Wisdom allows me to understand my limits. Are those limits humbling to accept? Yes! I don't always understand the whys, but I can rest easier knowing that God knows what he's doing. Notice I said "easier" and not "easy." Sometimes, no matter how much we embrace God's wisdom, our human reaction of anxiety kicks in. When we are anxious, our minds are usually somewhere in the past or the future, and some of us may become so anxious that it leads to a panic attack. Personally, I have had many panic attacks, especially during my high school years, and I used to be ashamed of myself because of them. Over time, I realized that my anxiety was a normal, human reaction. However, I recognized that I needed to find a way to handle it better. Over time, when the panic started to hit, I started giving all of my concerns to God. This didn't necessarily erase all my fears, but over time, I learned to breathe deeply, accept the anxiety as it came, and give it to God, trusting in his wisdom.

Anxiety about a million different things can creep into our lives at any given moment, and it is a natural result of any kind of trauma. While this is not an easy thing to contend with, there is a cure. In addition to the psychological solutions, the cure for our worry is to trust in the wisdom of God, a wisdom that is far, far greater than any of us can even begin to imagine.

Hindsight is really a wonderful gift. I have often looked back at my life, and in hindsight I better understand how God's plan has unfolded. I can look back and say, "So that's what you were doing!" It's not the way I would have gone about it, but from where God sits, it makes perfect sense. By trusting in God's wisdom, I'm able to let go of the parts of my life that I have no control over. He knows what he's doing, even if I don't have a clue.

We may understand only when he calls us home to heaven one day. God has a plan, a plan greater than our own. In his wisdom, he knows where we are being led.

Prayer

Dear Lord, please grant me the grace of knowing when to let go. Help me to place all my trust in your great wisdom, and may my experiences help me to grow in knowledge and wisdom so that I may be more compassionate toward the sufferings of others.

Embracing Grace

Jesus is my strength. Jesus is my rock. I trust his wisdom and his will in my life. (Mother Angelica's motto)

Embracing a Grateful Heart

What is something that is sure to cheer you up (even just a little) after a difficult day?

_____

_____

_____

_____

One Small Step: Make a List

I really enjoy making lists. I make shopping lists, to-do lists, lists of ideas, and so forth. Oftentimes, my kids wind up accidentally using my beautiful lists for their artistic creations, but that's beside the point. Lists can be very helpful in organizing our thoughts and ideas.

Have you ever created a list of positive, concrete, achievable goals? Try it. There's no need to overwhelm yourself with big things (such as a career change). Start with smaller, short-term goals that will help you to begin your journey and help to build a more positive view of yourself. For example, a goal might be to spend fifteen minutes a day exercising. Another goal might be to talk to yourself in a positive way for five minutes every day. Yet another goal might be to pray the Rosary every day for a week. Whatever you decide on, I recommend making a list and then placing it in a place where you will see it frequently. Choose one goal at a time (maybe one a week), and when you feel ready, add another.

Questions for Reflection

How has your experience with sexual abuse changed your character?

_____

_____

_____

_____

_____

_____

What is some insight you have gained?

_____

_____

_____

_____

_____

How have your experiences with sexual abuse allowed you to better understand yourself? Have they allowed you to better understand others?

_____

_____

_____

_____

_____

PERSEVERANCE

Regardless of what you feel, regardless of what you think is true, the reality is that God believes in you. If he did not, he would not have created you, he would not have gifted you, and he would not sustain you. You are a precious treasure to God, and he believes in you. Grace is the evidence that God believes in you. Any time you exercise any of the virtues, or the fruits and gifts of the Holy Spirit, you do so because God believes in you enough to give you the gift of hope, or wisdom, or fortitude, or counsel, or knowledge. ... God believes in you.

— Dr. Gregory Popcak, *The Life God Wants You to Have*

Dear Friend in Christ,

Today, God offers you the gift of **perseverance**.

With God's grace, you have accomplished a lot. You survived. You're here. You're still standing. You're still fighting. You're still striving to heal. You have persevered. Do you know why you have come this far? Because God believes in you. Because he is giving you the gifts you need to heal. You have been so brave.

I know you don't always feel strong, and God's presence is not always immediately apparent. Life can so often feel like a giant roller-coaster ride, and this is especially true with healing. You're up, you're down, you're here, you're there. Sometimes you may feel as if you are hanging on to the roller coaster for dear life but also desperately trying to trust the conductor (while screaming your head off in terror). So often I have wished that ride would slow down. So often I have been reminded to turn to God in prayer and ask for just a little respite — a calmer, gentler ride. Despite the twists, turns, highs, and lows, I wanted so badly to see what would come at the end, and so I held on. I encourage you to keep holding on.

You will surely have your share of doubts. You may be kept awake many a night by the ruthless pull of anxiety and fear. Is it worth going to school and struggling through yet another day? Are all the therapy sessions worth it? Is facing your rapist at a trial worth it? What is it all for? What are you gaining from it all? Where are you going? What is going to become of you? Those nights may seem never ending. However, the light of Christ is within you. He is there to offer you hope, strength, and perseverance.

Have you ever felt as if you're observing someone else's life, but it's actually your own? I often felt as if I was looking in a mirror but not completely recognizing the person staring back. I would think to myself, was I really raped? Is my life really in as many pieces as it seems to be? Happier memories seemed like a lifetime ago, and I caught myself wondering if I had just imagined them. What happened to the innocent, carefree little girl who used to plant sunflower seeds and eagerly wait for them to grow? What happened to the child who used to look forward to the dawn of each day? Where was the trusting girl who had once held certain individuals (such as priests) in high esteem? That child might seem like someone else from another lifetime. But, even as I looked in the mirror, I knew this was me, and as strange as she often seemed, she needed to cling to God's grace and patiently persevere in healing.

God's gift of perseverance can give you the drive to forge ahead. Perseverance is the gift that will keep you trudging along the path even on days when you feel like giving up and abandoning the journey. Deep down within you, there is hope that things will get better. Trust that God has a plan that will work itself out in due time, even if you can't see it. One day you will look back and realize just how much perseverance God granted you. Whether there is a defining moment in which you recognize that gift or you simply look back and realize how far you've come, God is giving you the grace to keep going.

During my senior year in high school, my grades were not stellar and my college prospects were slim. My time and energy were primarily focused on the impending trial and frequent therapy sessions. It was apparent to my parents and teachers that I was overwhelmed and hanging on by a thread. My school guidance counselor gave me a choice: finish the year out, or take a break and begin senior year again next fall. For a brief moment, a part of me wanted to take her up on the second offer. I desperately wanted a break from school. It wasn't a terrible place, but I was tired of getting teased for my frequent fainting spells, of worrying about homework and due dates for assignments and projects, of feeling as if I didn't fit in, of peers finding out about my rape. On the other hand, I just wanted to get high school over with.

There are many things I've learned from my parents for which I am grateful, but if there's one thing I have particularly learned from them, it's perseverance, especially in hard times. My mother had an especially difficult childhood and yet persevered. My dad had also overcome various obstacles and was led closer to Christ. The lives of the saints came to mind, especially my old friend Saint Thérèse. She suffered. She felt weak and even hopeless. However, she clung to her faith, allowing it to guide her and give her strength to persevere to the very end. Healing suddenly became to me not a question of "Will I do it?" but rather "How will I do it?"

Lo and behold, I did get through my senior year. My grades weren't my dream grades, but I had done my best. When I nervously walked across the stage at graduation, I thought, "Thank you, Lord!" I had had a lot of wonderful support from my family and friends, but I also knew that, without Jesus in my life and in theirs, I never would have gotten through. He gave me the graces I needed, and he gave my family the graces they needed to help me. Receiving that diploma was like being handed the moon, but even more amazing was the knowledge that I had persevered through what had felt almost impossible. God believed in me even when I didn't believe in myself. God knew to be possible what I sometimes thought to be impossible. With his grace, united to him, I was enough.

That girl in the mirror found hope through perseverance. Hope made persevering worthwhile. Perseverance goes hand in hand with hope. The Merriam-Webster dictionary defines "perseverance" as "persistence in doing something despite difficulty or delay in achieving success." There's a lot to overcome when you have suffered. Healing takes time, patience, and grace. Healing requires our focus, faith, and trust in God. Persevering means refusing to give up, no matter what setbacks you face. It means weathering the raging storm at sea, allowing Christ to be at the helm of the ship.

If you are striving to move forward despite your setbacks, fears, and whatever else, then God is giving you the gift of perseverance. Just as we get better at something by practicing it, so "the testing of [our] faith produces steadfastness" (Jas 1:3). When our faith is tried, we learn to rely more on Christ, who lives within us. That reliance on him helps us to forge ahead, making us stronger and more determined. That is something to celebrate! As the apostle James says:

> Count it all joy, my brethren, when you meet various trials, for you know that the testing of your faith produces steadfastness. And let steadfastness have its full effect, that you may be perfect and complete, lacking in nothing.
>
> If any of you lacks wisdom, let him ask God, who gives to all men generously and without reproaching, and it will be given him. But let him ask in faith, with no doubting, for he who doubts is like a wave of the sea that is driven and tossed by the wind. (Jas 1:2–6)

You show perseverance every time you get out of bed, especially after a sleepless night. Perseverance gets you through the day and helps you to look forward to the next day, knowing that brighter days are ahead. Perseverance is the reason you continue to seek help. Perseverance allows you to hold on to faith, trusting that God is always with you in the ups and the downs. You persevere because you have hope. You have hope that you can heal. You have hope of a brighter future. You have hope in the joy of the Resurrection, in the knowledge that God always brings some kind of good out of suffering.

You can trust him on that. Don't listen to the lies of the devil, that no good will come of your present suffering. In the words of Mother Angelica: "There is nothing that pleases Satan more than to see all of God's children confused and resentful about the suffering in their lives. Satan doesn't want you to gain grace and transformation from suffering; he wants you to rebel against God in defeat, to give up, and to throw away your potential for holiness." You can have hope that if you just keep plugging along, dawn will break and bring an end to the darkness of the night you face. Keep going even when it's hard.

Mother Angelica talked about persevering in times of doubt or when our faith is feeling weak or being attacked. Her advice? "Persevere in prayer now." Padre Pio explains more: "Don't worry to the point of losing your inner peace. Pray with perseverance, with faith, with calmness and serenity."

One prayer I highly recommend is the Rosary. Though some people may find the Hail Marys to be very repetitive, I find that repetition to be quite calming. The prayers of the Rosary can be learned by heart and, in moments of anxiety, can help to keep you grounded and focused. Many a night, in the midst of battling the anxieties of an overwhelmed mind, I have grabbed my rosary and prayed the Hail Mary over and over again. (If you're struggling to pray at all during this season, or need some tips on prayer, see appendix I.)

I want to share a powerful prayer with you that Our Lord gave to Saint Faustina as part of the Chaplet of Divine Mercy. This prayer always brings me great peace when I am struggling to keep going in the midst of difficulties: "Eternal God, in whom mercy is endless and the treasury of compassion — inexhaustible, look kindly upon us and increase Your mercy in us, that in difficult moments we might not despair nor become despondent, but with great confidence submit ourselves to Your holy will, which is Love and Mercy itself. Amen."

Pray, accept God's gifts, don't despair, and persevere. God's got this.

Prayer
Lord, thank you for helping me come this far. Thank you for believing in me even when I have not believed in myself. Please grant me the gift of perseverance. May I always look to the future with hope.

Embracing Grace
I can rise above the challenges I face and achieve my goals of healing.

Embracing a Grateful Heart
Did you accomplish something recently or in the past that you feel good about?

_____

_____

_____

_____

One Small Step: Have a Laugh
Facing the reality of sexual abuse is not an easy thing to do. You might be feeling sad, anxious, fatigued, vulnerable, and depressed. However, you continue to persevere because you know that there is a beautiful future ahead of you. When we think of healing, we may automatically think of therapy, prayer, counseling, and certain self-care techniques. However, there is one self-care technique that a lot of people may not think of that comes free of charge and is accessible to all: laughter. I know, I know. Laughing may be one of the last things you feel like doing right

now. You might feel as though you will never again find amusement in anything. But laughter is so important. Laughing can release positive hormones that can help you relax and feel better.

Everyone has a different sense of humor, and what makes me laugh might not make you laugh, but I encourage you to try it anyway. You can start by looking up memes that you think might be amusing or watch a favorite comedy movie. Personally, I love to watch humorous videos of silly animals on YouTube. Whatever it may be, remember that it's okay to laugh sometimes. It feels good and is a God-given gift in and of itself.

Questions for Reflection

How can your perseverance in suffering lead to greater hope?

_____

_____

_____

_____

_____

_____

What character traits do you have that can help you to persevere?

_____

_____

_____

_____

_____

What are some of your goals, and what do you need to do to achieve them?

_____

_____

_____

_____

_____

_____

PATIENCE

*Have patience with all things, but chiefly have patience
with yourself. Do not lose courage in considering your own
imperfections, but instantly set about remedying them —
every day begin the task anew.*

— Saint Francis de Sales

Dear Friend in Christ,

Today, God offers you the gift of **patience**.

While you are healing, you will experience good days and
bad days and everything in between. Some days you will feel in-
vincible, and other days you will feel as if you're right back where
you started. As difficult as it is to feel as if you've gone ten steps
backward, those feelings are normal. During those times, it is
especially important to allow yourself some grace and to accept
God's gift of patience.

Let's face it: The world around us isn't usually a very patient
one. We desire easy, quick fixes for just about every issue we face,

101

and instant gratification for the things we want. Yet, so often we discover that things don't happen as quickly as we want them to. We don't get what we want simply because our minds have had a sudden inspiration. I couldn't wait to be done with the trial against my rapist, but I had to prepare with time and patience. I was impatient to heal, and yet I discovered that healing takes God's gifts of strength, perseverance, and patience. Over the years, there have been so many days on which I've felt the urge to scream toward the heavens, "I want it now!" in a near-perfect imitation of Veruca Salt from *Charlie and the Chocolate Factory*. Veruca learned the hard way that wanting everything now isn't always wise.

The greatest saints would probably tell you that strength in suffering produces the most patience. All of God's gifts seem to build on each other, don't they? We find the gift of patience through the gift of perseverance, a gift that comes from strength. Patience leads to even more gifts. As Venerable Fulton Sheen said in his book *Way to Inner Peace*, "Tribulation tries the soul and in the strong it develops patience, and patience, in its turn, hope, and hope finally begets love."

Just as there is no limit to God's grace and patience, there is no time limit to healing. We're all different, and we all need to allow ourselves the time to heal, however long that might be. For me, one of the most difficult parts of the healing process was (and still is) being patient. When I entered therapy and began facing my past head-on, part of me thought in terms of how society around us thinks — that everything would improve right away, drastically and dramatically. How disappointed I became when I realized that my pain wasn't going away overnight. I had to accept that I had been through something extremely traumatic, something that goes against human nature, and it was life changing. I needed to live patiently while I slowly rebuilt my life and got to know the new me.

Patience means being able to take two steps forward and one step back. Patience means allowing yourself grace when a bad day comes and you feel as if the weight of the world is on your shoulders. Memories take time to process; fears take time to work through; and Triggers take time to disarm.

Triggers: the word alone makes my skin crawl, because nothing could have prepared me for how intense triggers can be. Triggers are side effects of any kind of abuse. Each person's triggers may be different — perhaps it's a smell, a place, or a person that causes us to freeze, to feel as though we are right back in the time and place of the abuse. Triggers cause us to react as if the abuse is still going on. They can come on fast, unexpectedly, and pack more intensity than a raging hurricane. Sadly, you probably already know exactly what I'm talking about.

Developing healthy coping mechanisms can help put the trauma in the past, where it belongs, instead of front and center all the time. Do you suffer from a particular trigger or triggers? It took perseverance and patience to identify each of mine and address them. Addressing them all at once was just too much, but taking them one at a time allowed me to work through them reasonably and thoroughly, therefore disarming their ability to affect my daily living. Over time, instead of freezing, I was able to use the coping mechanisms I had learned: to breathe, pray, and talk myself through the trigger. I sometimes still succumb to memories. I am still triggered from time to time. Triggers come from memory, and though the memory of abuse fades, it is never fully erased. Just because you may encounter a bad memory or experience a trigger does not mean that you have failed. God's gift of perseverance will help you keep going even after a flashback, and the many coping mechanisms available to you can help reduce the intensity of those memories and triggers.

The trauma associated with sexual abuse doesn't completely disappear just because you've talked it out or gone through extensive therapy. The pain of the wound does heal over time, but a scar will always remain. The reality is that sexual abuse is something that may need to be addressed as your life changes and the abuse affects you in different ways. I worked through my abuse as best as I could, based on the situation I was in at the time — a high school and college student. Then I had to address it as my circumstances changed, because how it affected me changed. Marriage, for example, caused me to address my intimacy issues. My first full-time job working in the mental-health field added another layer of healing. Now, as a wife and mother, I need to address the issues that present themselves in my current state in life. As long as I address and accept them as they come, I know I'll be okay. Quashing them, ignoring them, has never been helpful — believe me, I have tried. The memories, the triggers, will only resurge again, whether emotionally, psychologically, or spiritually. Accepting the lifelong process of healing requires patience with ourselves and with those around us.

Everything happens in God's time. The trouble for us is that we don't understand God's time. We may trust in his promise that good will come out of the bad, but it sure is tough waiting around for it to happen, isn't it? God's ways are different from ours; his timing is different from our time. In Saint Paul's Letter to the Romans, he says, "Rejoice in your hope, be patient in tribulation, be constant in prayer" (12:12). In other words, hold on to hope and keep going.

From Saint Teresa of Ávila we receive this wise advice: "Let nothing disturb you, nothing frighten you; all things are passing; God is unchanging. Patience gains all; nothing is lacking to those who have God: God alone is sufficient."

Feeling stuck in a season of waiting is very challenging, but change is a process, and healing requires some amount of change. We can choose to wait with frustration and misery, or we can trust in God's timing with hope and rest easier knowing that he is guiding us as we work on our problems. As Mother Angelica once said, "Patience is adjusting your time to God's time." His timing is different from ours since the concept of time means nothing to God.

Our culture wants instantaneous results. Think about how easy it is to get answers to the most random questions — it's as simple as tapping a few keys. Unfortunately, healing doesn't work that way. But please let me reassure you: It gets better! It truly does. The wounds do and will heal. However, it takes time. It takes dedication and trust in God the Father. I also want to encourage you to look forward with hope but not to get stuck in the thought process of "Things aren't too good now, but maybe they will be one day." We have to live in the moment, face things as they come, and avoid worrying about the past, the present, and the future all at once. I've had lots of those days when I've just had to put everything else aside and allow myself to grieve. Some days can get challenging, and when they do, it's okay to slow down and remind yourself that there will be improvement with time. You will inevitably worry from time to time, but you don't need to get bogged down with worrying about things that haven't happened yet. Healing will get easier! Always cling to the knowledge that tomorrow is a new day. You will not be stuck in this seemingly endless roller-coaster ride forever. It's important to strike a balance between being content with today while looking forward to improving in the days ahead.

Sometimes, it's easy to remind everyone else to be patient. I know that I often find myself reminding people around me that results don't happen overnight. Have you ever decided one day that you're going to eat really healthfully or exercise, but you feel discouraged when you don't see any results after just a few days? I remember getting a kick out of a commercial (I think it was advertising a gym) that shows a man frantically running around the room once. Then, eagerly and with expectation, he jumps onto a scale to weigh himself. His face falls when he realizes that his weight hasn't changed at all after his one lap around the room! Clearly, he has very little patience and is getting easily discouraged by the fact that he isn't seeing instant results. He just put his all into that run around the room. And for what?

As with health and fitness, weight loss, a project, a goal, or learning a sport or a musical instrument, you have to patiently work at it, practice it, and gradually you will get better. You will develop the proper techniques that work for you. So it is with patience in healing. Restoring your mental and emotional health takes practice. It takes time.

It's also important to find patience with your support system. This is an important part of showing kindness, as we talked about earlier. I had to learn that the people around me who hadn't been victims themselves didn't truly understand what I was going through. They were figuring it all out right along with me. When my husband and I were first married, I had to be extremely patient while he got used to my triggers and to my ups and downs. It was so important for him to learn and for me to be patient with him so he could be a good support. We all need help carrying our crosses sometimes — even Jesus needed help carrying his cross to Calvary. Sometimes frustration takes over, and you probably think to yourself, "It's easier if I just do it myself." I strongly urge you to show patience to those people who are trying to help you and to accept help when it is offered.

Let me remind you that God is always waiting for you with outstretched hands. He is so patient, and he's willing to be by your side for as long as it takes, and then some. He will never leave you, and he will never give up on you.

Prayer
Dear Lord, please grant me the strength to persevere and to have patience throughout the healing process. Please help me to accept that change will not happen overnight and that, with prayer and patience, things will get better.

Embracing Grace
I am patient with myself and allow myself to heal even as the circumstances in my life change.

Embracing a Grateful Heart
What is a food that you particularly enjoy?

_____

_____

_____

_____

One Small Step: Spending Time with Jesus

Even in the best of times, life can get hectic. We feel as if we are running in a million directions. We're a go, go, go culture. Sometimes, you just need a few moments to collect your thoughts, pray, and focus on Our Lord and on the journey you are on. If you can, spend a few moments in church before Jesus in the Blessed Sacrament. Find a few moments to just sit, close your eyes, quiet your mind from the endless to-do list, and listen to him speaking deep within your heart. Even if you don't feel, see, or hear anything, offer yourself to him anyway. Many times I have been too overwhelmed and anxious, and my mind such a whirlwind, that the best I could do was to say, "Lord, I'm here. I offer myself to you as I am."

Questions for Reflection

When you feel impatient, how does it manifest itself in your actions? Do you lash out, become angry, resentful, withdrawn, etc.? How does this affect you? The people around you?

_____

_____

_____

_____

_____

_____

Is there a situation in which you particularly struggle to be patient with yourself (or with others)?

_____

_____

_____

_____

_____

_____

SELF-COMPASSION

Christ, who is your life, is hanging before you, so that you may look at the Cross as in a mirror. There you will be able to know how mortal were your wounds, that no medicine other than the Blood of the Son of God could heal. If you look closely, you will be able to realize how great your human dignity and your value are. ... Nowhere other than looking at himself in the mirror of the Cross can man better understand how much he is worth.

— Saint Anthony of Padua

Dear Friend in Christ,

Today, God offers you the gift of **self-compassion**.

When you look at everything you need to do, healing sometimes seems like an impossible task, doesn't it? Facing the truth of your experiences and acknowledging your feelings of weakness, vulnerability, and grieving loss are difficult. It's life changing. Addressing your trauma while trying to carry on with your day-to-day tasks adds to the struggle. You carry a heavy burden, a burden that you don't have to carry alone, a burden from which you are allowed some respite. When your burden seems heaviest, you need to allow yourself grace and do what you can, trusting that God will take care of the rest. During these times, God most wants to give you the gift of self-compassion.

Do you find it easier to show compassion to others than to yourself? Wanting to take care of ourselves can feel a little selfish, but showing proper respect for yourself and treating yourself with dignity actually honors God. God sees you as valuable. He created only one of you. You owe yourself the same respect that our Creator gives you. Showing yourself the same kindness and compassion that you would show others who are struggling is okay.

Shame is one of the most damaging results of sexual abuse, affecting how we view ourselves and how we interact with those around us. Shame causes low self-esteem and lack of confidence. When we are full of shame, we tend, even sometimes unknowingly, to push people away. Handling triggering situations can be burdensome and can make relationships (particularly intimate ones) even more strenuous.

You've probably spent a fair amount of time criticizing yourself and tearing yourself down. I know all too well how prevalent those lies in our minds can become and how difficult it is to accept truth over the lies. Despite what those lies may be trying to get you to believe, you are worthy of compassion, kindness, and love. Believe it or not, as Christopher Robin once said to Winnie-the-Pooh, "You are braver than you believe, stronger than you seem, and smarter than you think."

Try not to be so hard on yourself. I know how challenging this can be. Remember, healing isn't a race. God doesn't expect you to break into a sprint. He's not standing off to the side, impatiently tapping his foot and checking his watch in annoyance. He's not going anywhere, and neither are his gifts, if you are willing to accept them as he offers them. Our Lord is ever so gently urging you forward. He's helping you up the steep hills and over any obstacles in your path. Stop when you need to stop. You don't have to be tough all the time. You don't have to put on a happy face every moment of the day or explain to every person you meet what you are going through. Be kind to yourself. You are human, and healing takes time. Finding the things that work for you on your healing journey also takes time. There is no one-size-fits-all approach.

Acknowledge to yourself that you've been through trauma and that you're suffering. You are allowed to grieve, to face the emotions, and to process the memories. You're going to have bad days when you feel miserable, and that's okay. You may have good days when you feel as if you can take on the world. That's okay too. Healing is like that. Some days you feel as though you're moving forward, whereas other days you feel as though you're moving backward. There's no need to force yourself to keep a stiff upper lip. Be gentle with yourself, as Our Lord is being gentle with you.

What are some ways you can show yourself self-compassion and gentleness? The One Small Step sections throughout this book provide some suggestions you may find helpful. Some other ways to be gentle with yourself include: taking a rest day, doing something you enjoy, celebrating small accomplishments, not comparing yourself with others (remember, we all heal differently), talking to yourself in a positive way, and allowing yourself to say no so as not to take on more than you can handle. There is a cost to pay if you do not listen to your needs. Dealing with the effects of sexual abuse is difficult in and of itself, but your healing will only be all the harder if you are not properly caring for yourself in mind, body, and spirit.

Know when you're trying to do too much. Being strong doesn't mean that there is a need for you to put on the illusion of constant, superhuman strength. Sometimes being strong means recognizing and admitting, "I'm trying to do too much. I need to rest." There is strength and wisdom in being able to recognize when enough is enough.

Personally, I have a tendency to go, go, go until I can't handle anything else thrown at me. Then the volcano that has slowly been building within me explodes. I particularly became aware of this tendency during my college years, after the trial was over. I figured, "Hey, it's all over now!" and so I embarked on the journey of being a normal college student. I took on one too many classes my freshman year and had one too many commitments, and I left little time for prayer and reflection. I quickly learned that while keeping busy can be a good distraction at times, it can be such a distraction that we ignore things that shouldn't be ignored. The things we try to ignore will rise to the surface at one time or another. If any of my friends had been in the same situation, I would have told him or her, "Slow down. You're trying to do too much!" The truth is, I just wanted to feel normal. I wanted to fit in with the world and not feel like such a stranger to everyday, human life. I didn't want to feel like such a stranger to myself, for that matter.

Here's what I realized over time: I was still me, but I had changed. I needed to practice patience in getting to know the new me. I needed to have patience with myself, with the healing process, and with those around me who were trying to help and support me. Most of all, I needed to be compassionate toward myself. I didn't need to force myself to do it all. Instead, I needed to treat myself with love, kindness, dignity, and respect, to be more mindful of my limits, and not to push myself beyond my capability.

Do what you can. God will take care of the rest. Our culture has so many unrealistic expectations about healing. As much as I enjoy some Hallmark movies, rarely does anything in life go quite so smoothly as in those movies. In real life, a difficult situation doesn't wrap itself up in an hour or two. Rarely is there an all-wise Grandpa Walton–type person in our lives who knows just what to say at just the right time. Life isn't a neatly wrapped box with a pretty bow. Even in the best of situations, life can be downright difficult. It is even harder when we suffer because of the sins of another.

We can easily fall into the trap of feeling as if we somehow deserved what happened. The truth is, no one deserves to be abused. I sometimes imagine myself looking in on my life as if I were a stranger — how would I treat that person? Being compassionate and kind toward others can seem so easy in comparison with showing ourselves the same dignity and respect.

How would Jesus treat you? By suffering and dying for us, Jesus showed greater compassion for all of mankind than anyone ever has or ever will. Our suffering became his. Our anguish and torment became his. If Jesus could show each of us such love and mercy and compassion, we are worth receiving that same love from ourselves.

Your innocence may have been stolen, but your purity was not. Perhaps you may feel as though your dignity and worth have been snatched away and are lost, but this is a lie. You still have dignity, and your worth in God's eyes is beyond what any of us can imagine. You are a priceless gem! The lies we tell ourselves are very normal reactions to the trauma we have undergone. I will continue to tell you that there is hope. Hold on to faith, trust in God, accept his graces, and you will heal. Those feelings of shame aren't going to go away overnight, but they can get better. Sexual abuse (or any kind of abuse, be it emotional, spiritual, or physical) does not define who you are. It has become a part of who you are, but it's up to you to allow God to make it shape you and not destroy you.

Shame can cause us to think we don't deserve love, kindness, dignity, and respect, but that's just one of the many lies Satan wants us to believe. You do deserve those things, from others and from yourself. God offers you so many precious gifts. In the Book of Psalms we read, "He heals the brokenhearted, and binds up their wounds" (147:3), and he desires to tend to you too. He is gently helping you to heal.

Prayer
Heavenly Father, there is no one more compassionate and understanding than you. Help me to be patient and compassionate toward myself.

Embracing Grace
I am gentle with myself and show myself kindness, patience, and respect.

Embracing a Grateful Heart
What is a scent you like that brings you comfort and relaxes you?

_____

_____

_____

_____

One Small Step: Learning to Be Mindful
We live in a hurried world, always rushing or being rushed. We've got places to go and things to do. When we're dealing with the aftereffects of a trauma like sexual abuse, the insanity of the world around us can cause us to feel rushed in our own healing. Take a small, relatively routine habit (such as brushing your teeth or your hair) and try slowing it down. Really concentrate on what you're doing in that moment. Think about how your body feels, and allow your five senses to bring you into the moment. I know it may seem silly to concentrate on something as mundane as brushing your teeth or your hair, but it's good practice for helping you to ground yourself in the present, especially when you're experiencing a flashback or being triggered by something. Often, when I am feeling triggered, I find something (however small) to focus on and utilize my senses to help bring my mind back to the present. I can remind myself, "I am safe. I am okay."

Questions for Reflection

Do you have a hard time showing yourself compassion and kindness? Do you tend to self-judge? If so, why do you think that is?

_____

_____

_____

_____

_____

_____

Do you find it easier to show kindness to yourself or to others? Why?

_____

_____

_____

_____

_____

What are some self-judgments you have placed on yourself? How can you turn those self-judgments into self-kindness?

_____

_____

_____

_____

_____

PART III

FINDING FREEDOM

Pause and Pray

Mother Angelica's Prayer for Inner Healing

Lord God, Father of all, we come before Thee today empty with our soul in need of healing. We need that confidence and hope that comes from Your Holy Spirit. Help us to realize Your love for us and to give that love to our neighbor. We need to rebuild and renew. There is in each of us something in our memory that keeps us from being compassionate and merciful. So deeply rooted are these gnawing resentments that they obstruct us from the good You have for us. We ask You to reach into each of our memories now and heal them. Touch that unforgiving spirit within us and drive it away, Father. We know You forgive us, but we find it so hard to forgive ourselves. Remove all the regrets of the past. Lord Father, we know You are present now and beg You to remove all of our guilt and make us new so we can be used by Your Son. Lord Father, reach in and heal us all and fill us with the love and compassion that surpass all understanding. Amen.

GRATITUDE

The secret of happiness is to live moment by moment and to thank God for all that he, in his goodness, sends to us day after day.

— Saint Gianna Molla

Dear Friend in Christ,

Today, God offers you the gift of **gratitude**.

God made you in his image, and you are beautiful. You are a valued child of God, and your identity is in your relationship with him. I love the verse from Song of Solomon that says, "You are all fair, my love; / there is no flaw in you" (4:7). If you don't believe those words now, you will one day.

Probably we have never met, but nonetheless I am grateful for your presence in this world. God created you to be uniquely and beautifully you, and he is going to bring good out of your pain. Through his healing power, your life will be transformed. I am grateful that you are choosing to journey down the healing path and grateful that you are allowing God to work in your life. You may not realize it, but that is a very precious gift that you give to the world. You may never know how your experience may become a source of healing for others.

Take a moment and breathe slowly and deeply. Think about where you've been and what you've overcome. Think about the gifts God has given you to help you get to wherever you are at this moment. Consider his glimmers of grace. How have they affected your life and aided your healing?

When we take a moment to ponder God's great goodness and allow ourselves to focus on the good in our lives, we can't help but experience tremendous gratitude. Gratitude is a beautiful gift. When we look at the world around us with gratitude, our eyes are opened to the beauty in and around us, despite our pain and suffering. Gratitude opens our hearts to experiencing joy, love, peace, and freedom.

I remember feeling a sense of loss after being abused, as if I lost of a part of who I was. I often felt disconnected from myself. I struggled to form any semblance of a rational thought, and no wonder — I was so busy facing each day as it came, and I focused on just putting one foot in front of the other. I was running on autopilot. When we're experiencing the grief that comes with trauma, life falls into a sort of rhythm that allows us to focus on doing what's vital, and not much else. Trauma takes center stage in our minds, and we can sometimes fail to see much else except what's staring at us from the spotlight.

Gratitude focuses on the positive, something that can be very difficult after surviving abuse, and helps put things into perspective. This does not mean that we deny the bad — we just learn to focus on the fact that there are good things happening in our lives. These are the glimmers, God's gifts. Making an effort to look beyond our grief helps us feel more human and more whole again. Gratitude brings hope and joy to the forefront.

Does this gift solve everything? Of course not, but it helps to plant the seeds of joy in our aching hearts. Having a thankful heart helps us to see things in a new light. During hard times, at first we may find ourselves thinking, "Nothing is going right! What is there to be grateful for? I have nothing to be positive about!" — as we stomp our feet and shake our fists at the heavens. Gratitude doesn't always come easy. In an article for *OSV Newsweekly*, Mary DeTurris Poust says that gratitude "requires action and determination to look for those moments of grace, even when they are hidden among the thorns of disappointment."

I vividly remember sitting on the back stoop of my house one day, feeling completely defeated, unwanted, neglected. Numb with grief and fear, my heart felt as if it had been shattered into a million pieces. While my friends and classmates were getting ready for the senior prom and graduation, I was preparing to face my rapist in a courtroom. My day had been particularly rough; I had suffered yet another fainting spell. I had passed out so often at that point (due to stress and anxiety) that my classmates teased me. Perhaps they didn't realize that their playful teasing was hurtful and caused me further embarrassment. I wanted to feel special, and, like any kid, I wanted to fit in. No one likes being the odd one out. I was envious of the kids whose lives seemed to be going in a fairly straight line. My strength was running low, and I had nothing left to give — even my tears seemed to have dried up.

My prayer on that afternoon was that God would offer me some respite. I desperately needed to know he was still there. "I don't need a big sign, Lord," I prayed, "just a small reminder that I'm not alone and that you hear me." A light breeze kissed my cheek, and the cheerful song of a wren pierced through my self-pity. Something faint awoke inside of me: a realization of the Creator and all of his beauty, of my uniqueness and that I, too, was God's creation. My life felt far from beautiful at that moment, and yet I realized that beauty was all around me in its simplest form. God's creation spoke of his love for me, as though to say, "You are my masterpiece, my daughter. I created all this, but you are worth far more than all this beauty that surrounds you." I became overwhelmed with a sudden appreciation for my uniqueness and the uniqueness of the story of my life. A rush of gratitude entered my heart as I recognized the good in my life: my beating heart, the breath in my lungs, a brain that could think, a heart that could love, the people who loved me, the support I had, a good education, the beauty that surrounded me, my faith … there was much to be grateful for. I was reminded of how far I had come in my healing journey. There was so much to look forward to, so much to hope for.

There's a scene in the 1960s cartoon *How the Grinch Stole Christmas* in which the bitter, resentful Grinch has a sudden realization about the true meaning of Christmas, and his heart literally swells with love and gratitude. Metaphorically, that's what happens to us when we open our hearts to gratitude. It helps our hearts to grow. As a result, we become more positive people, and finding beauty even in the midst of suffering becomes easier — not easy, but easier. One of the reasons I have included the "Embracing a Grateful Heart" section at the end of each reflection is to encourage you to practice living in gratitude every single day. This gift requires practice.

Even when we feel reassured of God's presence and grace, the real changes in our hearts don't always happen right away. They certainly didn't for me. We have to make a conscious decision to be fully present in each moment. Gratitude is something we practice and it is a good way to begin and end each day — thanking God for at least one grace or blessing from our day or from our lives. In his book *A Call to Joy*, Matthew Kelly tells us, "No other prayer will fill you with greater joy than a prayer of gratitude."

The switch from living in a mind that feels dark and hopeless much of the time to living in a mind full of more light, more love, and joy is truly a gift. When our hearts are more open to accepting God's glimmers of grace, gratitude opens our minds to a greater freedom and a more positive way of thinking than we could have ever thought possible. This mindset may not come naturally at first, as trauma can cause our minds to become wired to think negatively (a normal side effect). Again, I encourage you to practice, and over time, this will become easier.

God never promised a perfect life free from suffering. Jesus himself suffered. His mother, Mary, suffered. The saints suffered.

Yet one of the many things they had in common was gratitude. They gave thanks no matter what they were going through, even in the crosses they carried, because they trusted that God would use their suffering for good. Life is a precious gift. Growing in gratitude helps us to recognize that God, our heavenly Father, has given us so many gifts. A gift doesn't have to be elaborate; sometimes the most simple gifts are the most precious to us.

Today, accept God's beautiful gift of gratitude. Allow your heart and your mind to be opened to the glimmers of his grace and to accept his goodness with joy and love.

Prayer
Dear Lord, please help open my heart and mind to embrace your gift of gratitude. Help me to accept your gifts and to be grateful for them, and help me to share that gratitude with others.

Embracing Grace
I am filled with gratitude for the ability to heal.

Embracing a Grateful Heart
What is your favorite place to relax?

_____

_____

_____

_____

One Small Step: Practicing Gratitude
Gratitude is a big part of what this book is all about: recognizing and accepting God's gifts, even in the small events of life. In his book *God Help Me! This Stress Is Driving me Crazy! Finding Balance through God's Grace*, Dr. Gregory Popcak recommends that when you pray every evening, "write a list of five small blessings you encountered during the day. No matter how miserable your day was, look for those little moments and begin thinking of them

as brief caresses from the God who loves you enough to stop what he is doing and encourage you in whatever little way he can. Then acknowledge those small hugs with a simple thank-you." This was a very helpful practice for me, and still is.

If you're following the sections in this devotional, you're already recognizing things you are grateful for in "Embracing a Grateful Heart." On days when you are having a difficult time recognizing God's gifts, flip to "Embracing a Grateful Heart" on page 159, where you can write in the things you are personally grateful for. If you'd like, you can get a notebook and start a gratefulness journal in which you can write down a few things every day. There is beauty in simplicity, so don't be afraid to start with the small, simple things.

Questions for Reflection

Is gratitude a regular part of your life right now? Why or why not?

_____

_____

_____

_____

_____

_____

How can practicing gratitude help you to heal? If you aren't doing so already, are you willing to try practicing daily gratitude?

_____

_____

_____

_____

_____

When you think of the word "gratitude," what (or who) is the first thing that comes to mind? Who are the people and things you are most grateful for?

_____

_____

_____

_____

_____

LOVE

God loves each of us as if there were only one of us.

— Saint Augustine

Dear Friend in Christ,

Today, God offers you the gift of **love**.

Let me remind you of something: You are loved. You are a beloved child of God, and you are his masterpiece. He lives in you. You are valuable to him. He specifically created you to be the special and unique person that you are. In the Bible, we read, "Before I formed you in the womb I knew you" (Jer 1:5). Those powerful words are worth pondering. You weren't an afterthought. God planned to create you even before the moment you came into being in your mother's womb. He intentionally created each and every human life for a special reason.

You may think that suppressing or trying to forget feelings of sadness, anger, and fear is easier than facing them. You may be feeling damaged, worthless, dirty, unloved, and full of shame.

Perhaps at first glance it seems easier to pack all those yucky things into a box, lock it, throw away the key, and put that box into a dark closet, where you'll never have to see it again. I promise you that dealing with the pain is far better than attempting to hide it. I pray that you will continue to persevere through all this pain and finally come to see the truth: You are a precious child of God, and he loves you; nothing could ever make him stop loving you.

Whenever you question whether or not you are loved, or you doubt how much you are loved, take a moment to gaze at the crucifix. Do you see Jesus' wounds? His crown of thorns? The nails in his hands and feet? Can you imagine the suffering and humiliation he went through? That's how much you are loved.

You are precious.

You are loved.

You are God's masterpiece.

At my wedding in 2008, the officiant, a longtime priest friend of my family, spoke these words during his homily, "You are my love, you are my cross, you are my joy." As he said this, he held up a crucifix. My husband and I were led to understand that our individual crosses would become our shared crosses; our individual joys, shared joys; and our love, a shared love. This is just like our relationship with Christ. He shares in all our experiences, including our sufferings and joys. When we unite our lives to Jesus, we are fully united in love to him. After all, God is love.

I used to dread Holy Week somewhat because it felt so somber and depressing. After my experience with sexual abuse, I began to appreciate that week. When I was at my lowest, when I could hardly stand myself and was overcome by the devil's lies concerning my worth, Holy Week reminded me of God's love for me. In reflecting on Christ's suffering and death, I was reminded of the value of my life. My life had purpose — to be loved, to love God in return to the best of my ability, and to share that love with others. Condemning and hating myself had become like second nature, but God's love broke through like a ray of sunshine on a cloudy day.

We all have a choice: to respond to suffering with anger or with grace. Our vulnerability and fear of getting hurt can cause us to close our hearts to love. Even accepting the love of our Creator and of the people around us can be a struggle. Yet God's love heals. God's love allows for the joy of the Resurrection after the sorrow of Good Friday. By allowing our sufferings to be united to his, we can unlock the door to love.

I love what Mother Angelica had to say about the three theological virtues (faith, hope, and love): "Faith is what gets you started. Hope is what keeps you going. Love is what brings you to the end." One might say that love conquers all. Accepting God's unfailing love, even when we don't feel worthy, transforms us. God would never give up on any of us. Mother Teresa said, "God has not called [you] to be successful. He called [you] to be faithful." Isn't it a comfort to realize that he understands that we are not perfect? Isn't it reassuring to know that our heavenly Father will love us no matter what? Even when we ourselves feel completely unlovable, he loves us. Saint Teresa of Ávila left us these wise words, "Whenever we think of Christ, we should think of his love. It is with love that he has bestowed so many gifts on us. It is with love that God has given us such a sign and promise of his great love. Love gives rise to more love." As Saint Paul says in 1 Corinthians 13:13, love truly is the greatest of the theological virtues because, without it, faith cannot work.

The pastor of our church recently gave a homily that greatly resonated with me. He talked about choosing to run toward Christ. No matter how broken or how unworthy we feel, no matter our circumstances, Our Lord reaches out his arms, waiting for us to jump into them. Whenever you are tempted to run away from your past or from adversities, run toward him instead. He loves you so much, and his love is what gives you grace. Our Creator's love is what gives us all the gifts we need to heal. His love has no limits and never runs out.

God meets us all where we are. Human relationships can falter from time to time, but God never gives us the silent treatment or the cold shoulder. We have to make the choice to reciprocate that love or not. We must decide whether we will be open to and accept God's gifts. Nothing in this world can surpass the love that God has for each and every one of us. We can't even begin to fathom it.

Venerable Fulton J. Sheen shares some thoughts about God's love in his book *Life Is Worth Living*: "The love of God is something like the sun. Those who come very close to God enjoy both the Fire of his Love and the Light of his Truth." The truth is that God is love and his love for you is perfect.

I want to remind any of you reading this who may be practicing Catholics that you don't have to go far for proof of Christ's love. His love is there for you to experience as often as you choose. How is that possible? Simply put, Jesus is truly present in the Holy Eucharist, Body, Blood, Soul, and Divinity. This is the primary reason I have remained a Catholic despite the abuse I experienced at the hands of a Catholic priest and despite the evil that has been allowed to corrupt the minds and hearts of some of our leaders. In the words of Venerable Fulton J. Sheen, "The greatest love story of all time is contained in a tiny host." There is no greater gift that Jesus could have left us than that of himself. Consider that you can have Jesus himself in this most holy sacrament — not in any figurative sense, but in the actual sense that he is truly present and he is truly with you. Is there anything greater, more profound, and more mysterious than this?

Opening our hearts is not always easy. However, be reassured that God will meet you wherever you are. Pray. Pray that your heart will be opened to accepting his love and grace. Surviving isn't always easy — it wasn't for me. Sometimes you will feel weak and afraid. Yet, if you cast yourself at the feet of Jesus in prayer and allow your eyes to be opened to the beauty of his tremendous love for you and allow that love to envelop you, you will gradually find that you are able to move past the pain and to heal. Whenever you feel as though you are missing something in your life, consider that something may really be a someone. That someone's love surpasses all human understanding. That someone beckons to you and offers you grace upon grace every time, especially when you receive the sacraments (particularly confession and holy Communion). For me, just walking into a church can be physically painful at times. However, receiving Jesus in the sacraments never fails to provide my soul with an oasis in the midst of the desert.

Loving Jesus seems easy when things in our lives are going well, doesn't it? In those seasons, our relationship with Jesus often becomes so routine that we may take it for granted. Then, when adversity strikes, our side of the relationship may falter. What then? Do we blame God and shake our fist at him in anger? Or do difficult times remind us that we are merely human and therefore subject to the imperfect world, and so we need to rely on a power greater than our own? Do difficulties draw us closer to him or cause us to leave him?

Love is funny like that, isn't it? In any relationship, loving another human being seems so easy when life is even-keeled. When chaos strikes, we tend to lash out at those whom we love. Love, like so many other virtues, is not just a feeling but a decision. Anyone who has ever loved another human being understands that. You may not always like a certain person, yet you make the decision to love him or her anyway. My husband and I have certainly discovered that over the course of our marriage.

God's love never fails. Open your heart to give and receive love, and open your arms to receive the embrace of Jesus. His arms are outstretched on the cross. He patiently and lovingly waits for you.

Prayer
Loving God, please comfort me in my suffering. Help me to know that you are with me, and help me to open my heart to your limitless love and blessings.

Embracing Grace
God loves me. I am lovable.

Embracing a Grateful Heart
What do you consider to be your greatest accomplishment?

_____

_____

_____

_____

_____

_____

One Small Step: A Love Note to Yourself
I want you to write a love note to yourself. Yes, you read that right. Pretend, for a moment, that you are watching your life like a movie. Look at that person's life. Reflect on the difficulties they have faced. That person has been violated in the worst possible way by another human being. That person has been shamed, humiliated, and persecuted. That person has suffered tremendously. What do you want to say to that person? Write it down in a letter and keep it in a safe place. In moments when you're down on yourself, take out that letter and read it. When you're feeling pretty good, add to it if you want. Tell yourself all the wonderful things that make you special and unique.

If this is something you just aren't ready to do, then I encourage you to spend a bit of time each day reading God's love letter to you: the Bible. In her book *Beyond Sunday: Becoming a 24/7 Catholic*, Teresa Tomeo reassures us that "God's love letter will make you feel like you could not only run but win the Boston Marathon. It's that powerful." I don't know about you, but I'd say that's a love worth pursuing. Never forget how precious you are.

Questions for Reflection

Imagine having a day with Jesus, just you and he. If you could speak with Jesus today face-to-face, what would you say? What would he say to you?

_____

_____

_____

_____

_____

_____

What does it mean to you to hear that God loves you? Is God's love something you are able to accept? Why or why not?

_____

_____

_____

_____

_____

_____

Even if you don't feel God's love, how can you choose to respond to it?

_____

_____

_____

_____

_____

_____

JOY

Truly, truly, I say to you, you will weep and lament, but the world will rejoice; you will be sorrowful, but your sorrow will turn into joy.

— John 16:20

Dear Friend in Christ,

Today, God offers you the gift of **joy**.

You are worthy of happiness. You are worthy of feeling joy in your heart. Though we have never been promised a perfectly happy existence in this world, we can be assured that God desires to live in our hearts. He wants to give us moments of happiness, glimmers of hope, and the gift of joy.

Experiencing happiness and pleasure in the midst of terrible suffering can be very difficult, because "happy" goes against everything we are feeling when we are in pain. A part of us wants to experience pleasure, but another part has become so used to sadness that happiness feels foreign. There is a certain amount of retraining that we need to allow happy moments to enter into our lives. Positive affirmations and affirmations of gratitude are wonderful ways to combat the lies that the devil wants us to believe. Are you practicing yours every day? If you aren't already, I want to encourage you to start doing so. The devil wants us to feel anguished and hopeless, and he wants to manipulate our pain. He cannot stand to see us experience the joy that comes from accepting our worth as children of God.

Now, to be clear, we can't choose to be happy when something bad happens. We can't always control the immediate emotions of anger, sadness, fear, and so forth that overtake us; we are only human. But we do have control over what we do with those normal human emotions. Will you continually ask, "Why me?" or will you ask, "What can I do with this?" Will you trust the lies of the devil and give in to despair? Or will you trust in Our Lord's promise that "sorrow will turn into joy" (Jn 16:20)?

Although life isn't perfect, it can be peppered with beautiful moments — glimmers of God's grace. If we add those to our glimmer tanks, our tanks, over time, will become so full of happy moments that we will have a respite to turn to in moments of pain. These beautiful moments will become like droplets of cool water falling on your face on a blistering hot day. They are refreshing, reassuring, and pure, and they offer us hope and help us to live joy-filled lives.

You may be asking, "What is the difference between happiness and joy? Aren't they the same thing?" They can be connected, yes, but they are not one and the same. I find Dr. Gregory Popcak's explanation from his book *God Help Me! This Stress Is Driving Me Crazy!* to be extremely helpful:

> Happiness is a transient condition that comes and goes as it pleases. Joy, by contrast, being a gift of the Holy Spirit, is always a virtue, and though it is often accompanied by happiness, it is much bigger. Joy is the virtue that allows us to experience an all-encompassing sense of wonder and

awe at God's creation and the gifts he has given us. ... [Joy] always makes our burden lighter. ... When I make happiness my ultimate goal, I limit myself only to those activities and experiences that I find comfortable, leading to a very small life indeed. Joy, on the other hand, challenges us to live a more abundant life. It asks us to seek more, to try new things, to open ourselves to new experiences, and to expose ourselves to all of God's creation in all of its messy glory. Joy also draws us into deeper, more intimate relationships with others as it calls us out of ourselves and makes us more active players in our relationships, our community, and our world.

Happiness is fleeting, but joy lasts forever. To live with a joyful heart is to live with a faith-filled heart, a heart full of hope, trust, and peace. To live with joy does not mean we have to be happy all the time. That's impossible for any of us. To live a joy-filled life is to hold Christ within our hearts and souls. Joy is rooted in faith. The person who lives and walks by faith, who has hope and trust in Our Lord, who finds courage and strength in the Lord, who perseveres no matter what, ultimately experiences, as Matthew Kelly tells us, a "joy that cannot be extinguished by anything that happens."

Joy is what allows you to experience a deep, internal peace even in the midst of suffering.

Happiness and joy ultimately lead to even more happiness and joy. This is where gratitude especially comes into play. A truly grateful person feels more joy, experiences greater peace, and is led to greater healing. Joy helps us to grow and allows us to be more open to experiencing and expressing love.

Do we have to be happy with our present circumstances? Absolutely not! In fact, we shouldn't accept certain circumstances as they are without making any effort to change them, and the inner joy of Christ gives us the strength and guidance to help us to better navigate the unhappy difficulties we face.

Never feel discouraged when you feel anger, sadness, or confusion. Even after sifting through the memories and addressing the trauma, a certain sadness still remains. There is a sense of recognizing the loss of a part of your life and realizing how much you have endured. Quite understandably, you grieve your losses. Grief is a process that presents itself differently in each person and at different times. Hold tight to Our Lord, accepting his gifts. You are worthy of the joy and contentment that come from following Christ and allowing him to heal you.

So many things can prevent us from accepting happiness and joy. Feeling safe can be difficult after suffering abuse. Trusting is difficult. We often compare ourselves with others. We ask questions that we may never get the answers to. I know healing is a tough process, but you've got God in your corner. He's got this. We have to face our emotions, good or bad, as they come. We need support, a positive routine, and a prayer life. We need to practice self-care and show ourselves kindness and patience.

After suffering sexual abuse, you may feel alone, as though you're walking through a battlefield after a war has ended. You really have been through a war — in your mind, heart, and spirit. Allow yourself grace. Show the self-compassion you deserve. Despite what you've been through, despite the lies you may hear, despite the pain, confusion, and uncertainties, you are worthy of joy. God wants to live in your heart. Don't worry about feeling happy-go-lucky all the time. Such an expectation is unreasonable and unrealistic. Just remember that true joy comes from finding your worth as a child of God. Joy is not always a feeling but a peace that comes from God alone.

"May the God of hope fill you with all joy and peace in believing, so that by the power of the Holy Spirit you may abound in hope" (Rom 15:13).

Prayer

Lord, help me to recognize your presence and to find true and everlasting joy in you. Help me to see my worth as your child and to reflect that joy in my life, sharing it with those around me.

Embracing Grace
I am worthy of happiness. I am worthy of joy.

Embracing a Grateful Heart
Consider the traditions that may be a part of your life (Church traditions, family traditions, or traditions you've built in your own life). Is there one that you are particularly grateful for?

_____

_____

_____

_____

One Small Step: Take a Technology Break
Between TVs, phones, and computers, sometimes our lives seem like one big screen. Spending so much time plugged in often causes us to miss everything that's going on around us, including the good and beautiful things. I see teenagers and adults alike hanging out together — on their phones. People go for walks — while looking at their phones. We miss so much. Technology has certainly allowed us certain elements of pleasure in our day-to-day lives, but it can all too easily rob us of our opportunity to practice gratitude and experience joy.

Take a day to unplug from everything as best as you can. Go outside, go for a walk, gaze at the stars. Allow yourself to experience moments of happiness and peace, and pray that God will give you the strength to recognize him in those moments.

Questions for Reflection

When life doesn't go as planned, do you still feel joy, or do you turn away from God? Do you thank God for his blessings even when you are suffering?

_____

_____

_____

_____

_____

We all sometimes fall into the trap of believing "I'll be happy if such-and-such happens." How can this mindset be harmful and lead you away from joy?

_____

_____

_____

_____

_____

Have you ever met or known of someone who seems to be full of joy despite difficult circumstances? What do you think it is that causes that person to be so joyful?

_____

_____

_____

_____

_____

PEACE

Have no fear for what tomorrow may bring. The same loving God who cares for you today will take care of you tomorrow and every day. God will either shield you from suffering or give you unfailing strength to bear it. Be at peace, then, and put aside all anxious thoughts and imaginations.

— Saint Francis de Sales

Dear Friend in Christ,

Today, God offers you the gift of **peace**.

You may have had moments when you think no one could possibly ever understand your grief. Yet there is someone who completely understands. There is someone who has not only been with you during your sufferings but has also suffered right along with you. Yes, that person is Jesus, and we can bring all our pain to him. Dr. Gregory Popcak shares with us a beautiful reminder in his book *The Life God Wants You to Have*: "Though you are tired, frustrated, unfulfilled, and doubtful, trust in him and he will give you what you need. God believes in you." Read that again: "God believes in you." How awesome is that! God, the Creator of heaven and earth, the One who created you and loves you — he believes in you. He is, after all, your biggest cheerleader and also your biggest help. He desires that you come to him with every part of your life — the good and the bad.

Surrendering to God allows us to experience true and lasting peace. Many of us have a tendency to put our trust in things other than God. Perhaps some of these things produce comfort for a little while, but eventually, we are left feeling empty, alone, and searching. Many of the things that our society promises will be comforting are mere illusions. They don't bring peace, and they don't heal. We are left searching for something, although we don't always know what that something is. It's a deep-down feeling of a need that we can't quite explain. I want to remind you that there is one answer to that emptiness, and it's not a something. It's a someone: God.

Our world desires comfort. We talk about comfortable mattresses, clothes and shoes, furniture, even comfort foods. When pain strikes, there's often a solution for it; not that certain solutions are bad — far from it. Doctors, medicine, gidgets and gadgets, and so forth are truly blessings in our modern-day world. God has given us human beings the ability to perform certain tasks, to help others, to bless others with our talents. That's a gift. However, the commodities and comforts of life we have been blessed with tend to make us want to run from pain and suffering. This comes as no surprise, as no creature wants to suffer. Yet we often forget that there is a lot that can be gained through suffering. What is gained has a lot to do with each person's perception of suffering. Will suffering do us in, or will it bring about greater faith? This is the decision that each of us needs to make. This decision ultimately leads to hope of better things to come and help us persevere through difficult times.

Teresa Tomeo posted a piece adapted from her book *Beyond Sunday* on her website, with the heading "If God Is Your Co-Pilot, Change Seats." So often society encourages us to be "in control" of our lives, and yet, shouldn't it be God who is in control? Doesn't our strength come from him? Teresa goes on to say that allowing God to work in our lives "starts first with our complete 'yes' — when we get out of our comfort zone and let God take the wheel." Allowing our heavenly Father to take control of our lives takes faith, trust, and strength, but giving everything over to him ultimately brings us peace. Is surrendering to God easy? No. Is putting ourselves completely into his hands worth it? Yes!

God want us to be at peace. This doesn't mean that we will never get sad, angry, or depressed, and it doesn't mean that we will never worry. No matter what, every single human being experiences negative emotions at one time or another; it's a normal part of our humanness. There is so often a never-ending list of things to worry about, whether past, present, or future. However, low-level anxiety can be a source of motivation. Sometimes, worrying about certain things leads us to take action and improve something, making our lives better. Like all things, our anxiety can be crippling or reduced and developed as a strength. If we allow ourselves to live in the past or in the future, the devil will work hard to manipulate our worries so that they overtake us, thereby causing us to despair. Peace is found by living in the present, allowing Christ to do the driving.

To be clear, anxiety doesn't make you wrong or any less of a Christian. Anxiety makes you human, and, due to various circumstances, some of us are more prone to it than others. Our heavenly Father waits patiently to take all our anxieties and waits for us to put our trust in him. In moments of anxiety, I picture Jesus smiling lovingly and patiently at me, offering me his hand, and saying, "You're okay. I've got this. Trust in me. I'm taking care of you."

Anxiety is a difficult cross to bear, but having God at the center of our lives means that we have someone to take our anxiety to. There is peace in knowing that God will take care of everything. With God at the helm of the ship, you will not sink. He has brought you this far, and he will continue to guide you through the fog and storms. The waters will calm, and dawn will return. With God leading you, you have nothing to fear and there is hope, just as we read in the Book of Psalms: "For God alone my soul waits in silence, for my hope is from him. He only is my rock and my salvation, my fortress" (62:5–6).

I distinctly remember waking up one morning long ago and real-izing that my heart was no longer bitter. The result of a longer healing process, I was at peace with the past, the present, and whatever was to come. Despite the chaos in my life, despite the fact that I had suffered a lot, I realized how far I had come. Through acceptance and faith, through trust and hope, by recognizing the glimmers of God's grace, by embracing joy and gratitude, I recognized that, as often as I had wanted to do things my way, God's way had proved to be far better.

I will never understand how God works. We've heard that he works in mysterious ways, and it's the truth. Yet, we are called to surrender everything to him. In the Gospel of Matthew, Jesus says, "Come to me, all who labor and are heavy laden, and I will give you rest" (Mt 11:28). When in doubt, the best place to be is on your knees. As I have said before, we may not understand how God works, but we can trust completely in his guidance. "The peace of God, which passes all understanding, will keep your hearts and your minds in Christ Jesus. Finally, brethren, whatever is true, whatever is honor-able, whatever is just, whatever is pure, whatever is lovely, whatever is gracious, if there is any excellence, if there is anything worthy of praise, think about these things. What you have learned and received and heard and seen in me, do; and the God of peace will be with you" (Phil 4:7–9).

Peace springs from the knowledge that God's plan for us is al-ways good, even if we can't see that right now. With God's grace, we will rise from the tombs of our sadness, depression, anger, and grief. Realizing that our plans aren't always the best ones is pretty humbling, isn't it? Sometimes we are headed one way, but God gently nudges us down another path. This is when we especially need to pray to the Holy Spirit to show us the way and open our hearts to receive God's grace and accept his plan. Following God and accept-ing his will isn't always easy. Even Jesus struggled. We see him in the garden the night before he died, agonizing about the suffering that was to come. He was afraid, but he prayed and trusted. In faith, he surrendered himself to the will of the Father. He chose God's will over his own.

Peace erases that barrier that can so often come between us and God — the barrier that has us saying, "I want to do this my way." We can't do it our way, though, because our way isn't necessarily the right way. God's plan will always be better, and, as Matthew Kelly says, "Peace is the proof that God is present in your plans."

There is fear in not understanding how God works because, let's face it, we all want to gaze into a crystal ball and see the outcome of a certain situation. Trusting in God, understanding that he is ultimately in control, brings peace even if we can't see what he's doing. You can give anything and everything to God. That's not to say that we don't have to do our part; simply saying, "Jesus, I surrender myself to you," isn't always enough. We need to accept professional or spiritual help, or both, and there is absolutely no shame in that. Finding someone who can help us to integrate our spiritual and emotional needs is a crucial element in our healing. We are, after all, one in the Body of Christ, and each of us acts as Our Lord's hands and feet. Sometimes God allows certain people into our lives so that we may be helped.

By keeping our minds open to hearing God's voice and seeing his glimmers of grace, over time we may better know the way he has paved for us. It's pretty amazing when you think about it. God's way offers us joy, stability, and peace. Life can feel like a roller-coaster ride that causes us to hang on for dear life, and letting go of our worries and fears can be a struggle. However, God wants us to give ourselves completely over to him, and in doing so, we will find peace. What a relief it is to turn ourselves over to Christ and to be able to say, as Saint Thérèse of Lisieux said, "My soul is at peace, for long ago I ceased to belong to myself!"

Prayer

Dear God, please help me to surrender myself totally to you — my mind, body, and spirit, my pain, suffering, and difficulties. I know you understand it all. Please grant me the wisdom of the Holy Spirit to know where to go and what to do, especially in difficult situations. Help me to let go of my will and accept your will.

Embracing Grace
I invite the peace of God to enter into my life.

Embracing a Grateful Heart
What is something that you might ordinarily take for granted that you are grateful for?

_____

_____

_____

_____

One Small Step: Pray a Rosary
Aside from the Holy Sacrifice of the Mass, Catholics believe that the Rosary is the most powerful prayer. The Rosary is a powerful weapon against evil. There are lots of wonderful pamphlets and free resources explaining more about the Rosary, including how to say it. If you aren't already praying the Rosary, I encourage you to try it. The lives of Jesus and Mary are intertwined, and you see this especially through the prayers and mysteries of the Rosary. If, for any reason, you can't get through a Rosary in its entirety, try saying a decade (one Our Father, ten Hail Marys, and one Glory Be) at a time. Allow yourself to be united to the lives and love of Jesus and his mother. When you're up for more of a challenge, make it a goal to say the Rosary daily for a week, reflecting on each mystery and each prayer as best as you can. Through the power of this tremendous prayer, God will do great things in your life. Try it, and see where you are led.

Questions for Reflection

Is it difficult for you to surrender your life to God? Why or why not?

_____

_____

_____

_____

_____

How do you normally handle anxiety?

_____

_____

_____

_____

_____

How would you like to see yourself handle worries and fears that come your way?

_____

_____

_____

_____

_____

Are you able to turn to the Lord in prayer and allow him to enter into your suffering? If not, is that something you are willing to try?

_____

_____

_____

_____

FREEDOM

God wants everything, and in return he will give much more than we could ever imagine. God has a unique plan for each of us that is much greater than any plan that we could put together for ourselves. "No eye has seen, nor ear has heard, nor has it entered into the mind of man, anything as beautiful as what God has prepared for those who love him" (1 Corinthians 2:9).

— Matthew Kelly, *A Call to Joy*

Dear Friend in Christ,

Today, God offers you the gift of **freedom**.

You may not feel this way, but you are so brave. You are a warrior. When you opened your heart to accepting God's gifts, something really incredible happened. The first step you took led you to another step, which led to another and another. Somewhere along the path, you will be able to look back and realize just how far you've come. You will realize that Jesus has been with you the whole way, and he is still with you. No matter what changes come in your life, he will never leave. Our Lord calls each of us to invite him on our journeys and walk with him.

Journeying with Christ is not the easiest path to take. However, it is the only path that leads to true peace and freedom. Our world has this idea that freedom is being able to do whatever we want, when in reality, it is in surrendering ourselves to Christ that we become truly free. As we allow God's love and grace to permeate every facet of our lives, the devil's lies gradually lose control and we experience true and lasting joy and peace. Trauma doesn't have to be a life sentence of continual despair and grief. Healing doesn't happen overnight; it is often a long, painful process. But when you keep God close to you and open your heart to his gifts, amazing things happen. With God's grace, your healing can lead you to greater gratitude, joy, peace, love, and, ultimately, freedom.

We struggle to understand many things after abuse. I remember experiencing a sadness and a sort of stillness following my sexual abuse, especially after the adrenaline from coming forward and facing my rapist in court died down a bit. I didn't feel like myself anymore, and in many ways I had changed. I felt like a very different person from the girl who first entered that rectory. I struggled to understand the varying emotions that presented themselves, sometimes when I least expected them. One minute I felt okay, and the next I was collapsing into an exhausted, sobbing heap on the floor, wishing the ground would swallow me up. There was so much anger, fear, confusion, bitterness, resentment, and hatred in my heart that there was little room for much else. Those emotions festered and grew over time.

I was living in that deep, dark pit because all my energy was focused on shame and blame and on hating the man who had hurt me, and resenting anyone who had failed me in any way. I was slowly becoming a bitter, angry person. The hate constantly at the forefront of my mind overshadowed my joy. Really, it served no purpose and was only hurting me and those around me. Hate certainly wasn't leading me closer to God. Rather, my bitterness was drawing me further away from him and preventing me from fully experiencing goodness. Hate created a sort of wall that prevented me from experiencing God's love, peace, and joy in their fullness. I felt stuck.

One of my favorite book series is the trilogy *The Lord of the Rings* by J. R. R. Tolkien. In many ways, I can relate to the main character's emotions following his big adventure. After facing death, living through fear, danger, betrayal, and everything else in between, Frodo Baggins realizes that he can't return to the life he had before. He returns home and yet discovers that picking up the pieces and simply getting back to normal is impossible.

Frodo was a changed man (or hobbit, as it were), and he just couldn't lead the same carefree life he had once lived. He was understandably traumatized and needed to find his new normal. He was still Frodo but a different Frodo, made stronger and more resilient by his trials and suffering.

I felt a lot like this hobbit (minus the hairy feet). I was a changed person in more ways than one. So I asked God for the courage to let go of things that I knew I could not change. A time came when I realized that I had to let go of the bitterness, the guilt, and the shame while choosing never to let go of God. Letting go was a scary choice even to consider, because it seemed to go against all my human inclinations to hold on to the past and to hold on to the negative emotions. As always, God pulled through. Over time, with prayer and support and by repeating truth to combat the lies, I was able to recognize that I needed to release myself from the guilt and the responsibility I felt. In letting go, I found freedom. I found a stronger me — a me whose foundation lay in her faith in God, a me who could absolutely feel pain but could use that pain to drive myself forward, a me who was determined to hold on to hope and to persevere, no matter what. That's the power of the Holy Spirit for you.

God gives us all a really amazing ability to suffer while holding on to hope. We have the freedom to apply our faith to every circumstance that comes our way. Freedom allows us to choose hope, peace, and joy. Freedom allows us to work through all the emotions our suffering presents while still experiencing joy. We have the freedom to say yes to God, allowing him to enter into our healing.

We always have that choice. Teresa Tomeo reminds us that "God is a gentleman, and among his greatest gifts is the gift of free will. He doesn't force himself on us. Even though his plan is always the best plan, because as our Creator he created us for a specific purpose and mission, we have to have the buy-in, so to speak, on our end. It's up to us to have an open heart exercising our free will with a 'Yes, Lord.' " We are always given a choice.

When we accept this freedom, we experience a release from the bondage of sexual abuse. We break free from the chains of guilt, shame, and hate. I'm not for a moment suggesting that there will not be days when anger and resentment rear their ugly heads. I still experience feelings of guilt, shame, anger, and resentment from time to time. The good news is, you and I have the freedom to choose what to do when those emotions hit. Do we feed them and allow them to grow? Or do we combat them with truth and prayer and allow ourselves to grow in grace and virtue? Do we turn away from God? Or do we turn our mind and heart over to God and allow him to work in our lives?

At times, you are going to feel angry at God. He understands. He understands your anger, frustration, and resentment, and he feels your pain. Jesus experienced pain and humiliation in order to take on the sins of all mankind, so that we may experience freedom in him. Freedom of heart and mind does not mean forgetting, and it doesn't mean letting the person who hurt you off the hook. I still absolutely hold my rapist accountable. However, I no longer have any expectations about what he owes me. Anything he owes is to God alone. Achieving freedom takes love and trust in God, but it is possible.

Do you know what else? You are worth it! You deserve to be free from the darkness that binds you. You deserve to live in freedom as the precious child of God that you are.

Never forget that there is nothing that the devil wants more than to see you despair and give up. He will never give up in his efforts to bring you down into the pit of despair, hopelessness, fear, and anguish. One of the best quotes I have come across over the course of writing this book came from Dr. Gregory Popcak. He says: "There will be many times in your life when you hear Satan cackling in your ears and feel his hot breath sapping you of what little strength you have left. Fine. Let him have his moment. You will suffer, you will grieve, you will ache for justice that seems as if it will never come. But as you endure Satan's lash, the one question you must ask yourself over and over is this: When the worst of this is over, how will I live to make Satan sorry that he ever challenged me?"

The roller coaster of emotions is normal.
The pain you feel is normal.
You are a warrior.
You matter.
Your story matters.
You are a masterpiece of God.

The trauma you have faced should not define your life. Your pain and anguish do not need to steal your hope, your joy, or your inner peace. Strive to live in such a way that the devil, the father of lies, becomes enraged by the fact that you slipped through his fingers, because he wasn't able to exploit your suffering. Send him back to the dark abyss of despair where he came from! Choose to allow your suffering to lead you closer to the light — to God, the one who wants to free you from bondage. With freedom, you will fully experience God's glimmers of grace and many moments of healing and peace.

Hold on to your faith and never lose hope. Remember, with faith you can move mountains (see Mt 17:20).

Prayer
Lord, help me to rely totally on your love and grace, so that I may experience true freedom in you.

Embracing Grace
I release myself from any responsibility I have felt relating to my abuse. I release myself from hatred.

Embracing a Grateful Heart
What is a possession that you are most grateful for?

_____

_____

_____

_____

One Small Step: Declutter Your Life
There is a certain freedom that comes from simplicity. Today I encourage you to do a little cleaning. Is there any area of your home
that you can decluttter a little bit? How about your bedside table?
The kitchen counter? Your bedroom? Are you holding on to anything that brings back bad memories of the past (an article of cloth-
ing, a picture, a perfume)? Release those things. When you wake up
in the morning, you want to feel ready to take on the day, not feel
overwhelmed by the things around you. Material possessions can
overwhelm us because, let's face it, the more we have, the more we
have to take care of. Let go of the things you don't truly need, and in
doing so, you will provide more room for the people and things that
matter most.

Questions for Reflection

Do you struggle with feelings of hatred, bitterness, or resentment? Make a list of all the people, places, things, principles, and so forth that you feel resentment toward. Is your resentment leading you closer to Christ or further away from him? Does it make you feel free or not?

_____

_____

_____

_____

_____

Think deeply for a moment and consider how resentment and bitterness present themselves in your daily life. How do you think that letting go of those feelings can guide you toward freedom? How can faith help you with that?

_____

_____

_____

_____

_____

Make a list of the things you fear. How do these fears prevent you from experiencing freedom in Christ?

_____

_____

_____

_____

_____

Pray over these fears and resentments, and ask Our Lord to help you work through them.

EMBRACING GRACE

This page lists all the positive affirmations from the Embracing Grace sections of the reflections. In the additional space, I invite you to write your own affirmations that may be unique to you. Flip to this page when you need a little boost and to be reminded of your worth, dignity, and beauty in God's eyes. You are worthy of God's love and grace. You are a precious child of God. You are a masterpiece of God.

- I am worthy of receiving God's great gifts.
- I have faith that good will come out of my experiences. I can heal.
- I have hope in the future.
- Jesus, I trust in you.
- I am a precious child of God, and I am worthy of his love and grace.
- I deserve to be treated with kindness.
- I have courage to face my fears.
- I can do all things in [Christ] who strengthens me. (Phil 4:13)

- Jesus is my strength. Jesus is my rock. I trust his wisdom and his will in my life. (Mother Angelica)

- I am patient with myself and allow myself to heal even as the circumstances in my life change.

- I can rise above the challenges I face and achieve my goals of healing.

- I am gentle with myself and show myself kindness, patience, and respect.

- I am filled with gratitude for the ability to heal.

- I am worthy of happiness. I am worthy of joy.

- God loves me. I am lovable.

- I invite the peace of God to enter into my life.

- I release myself from any responsibility I have felt. I release myself from hatred, bitterness, and resentment.

EMBRACING A GRATEFUL HEART

Gratitude is like a muscle. In order to strengthen it, we need to exercise it. Gratitude is such a crucial part of healing, leading to greater peace of mind and greater joy. This page is for you to write down the things you are grateful for, so that you may focus on God's great graces and the blessings in your life. Just like the Embracing Grace page, this is a great place to come on days when you're struggling emotionally and unsure of God's presence in your life.

I have also provided some prompts to help get you started if you're feeling stuck. Don't worry if you struggle — you'll get the hang of it. Pray to the Holy Spirit for guidance and start exercising your gratitude muscle.

Gratefulness Prompts

- What are you thankful for today?

- What is something about nature that you are grateful for?

- Who is a person you are thankful for?
- What Bible verse do you like?
- Is there a saint you especially like?
- Is there a place you've been to that you have enjoyed?
- What kinds of art or music are you grateful for?
- Is there a particular song you enjoy?
- Do you have a favorite memory?
- Who is your favorite person?
- What makes you laugh?

ACKNOWLEDGMENTS

I have been blessed to have an incredible amount of support and guidance from some very special people. From the very beginning, God put into my life people who helped (and continue to help) mold my faith and bring me hope and inspiration. To those individuals, I offer my sincerest and most humble thanks.

To my dear mom and dad, the human beings on this earth who first loved me: You gave me the gift of life and planted the seed of faith in me from the start. Your guidance and spiritual strength have held me up on more than one occasion, and even though I no longer live under your roof, you continue to inspire and encourage me. For your guidance, example, prayers, and unending sacrifice, thank you. I love you.

To my husband, Alex, my best friend: You are my love, you are my cross, you are my joy! You were a surprise to me (and me to you, I'm sure). I am blessed to be sharing this journey with you and would not have come as far as I have without your support. I've watched you grow as a man, as a father, and as a Catholic, and you never cease to inspire and amaze me. You have overcome so much adversity in your own life, and yet you have persevered and allowed

Our Lord to work in your life and to transform you into the man you are. In a world where so many men run instead of fight, you stand a faithful warrior, clad in the armor of God. I am honored to be sharing this path with you.

To Teresa Tomeo, my sister in Christ: It was you who put me on the path to writing this devotional, and I am so grateful for your prayers, guidance, and support. I admire your courage and tenacity in always fighting to expose the truth. Even when it's tough to stomach and even when it hurts, you fight. You are truly an amazing woman, and the Holy Spirit is using you in amazing ways!

To Gail, my literary agent: My gratitude for your selflessness and encouragement is beyond words. You've believed in me even when I haven't believed in myself. Your unending support, prayers, and encouragement have inspired me more than you will ever know. I am blessed to have you in my life.

To my editor, Rebecca: Thank you for helping to give me and all survivors a voice! I am both honored and humbled that OSV had enough faith in my story to move forward with this devotional, and I am so grateful that God saw fit to put you in my life to help with this project.

To my dear lifelong friend Father Carroll; to my beloved Confirmation godfather, Father Higgins; and to my wonderful pastor, Father Chris: It is an honor and a privilege to have you faithful priests in my life. I have the greatest admiration and respect for you. For your prayers, guidance, example, and leadership, I thank you. Thank you for answering the call to serve Christ and his Church and for remaining faithful even in the midst of so much turmoil and evil. Your devotion and self-sacrifice are great, noble gifts. I hold you, my dear brothers, and your fellow priests in my heart and prayers in a very special way.

APPENDIX I

A Word on Prayer

Throughout the history of the church — in reading the Bible, in listening to the words of Jesus himself, and in listening to words of the saints and the Blessed Mother at her various apparitions around the world — we are over and over again encouraged to pray. Prayer is a crucial part of our relationship with God and an important part of the healing process. Sexual abuse deeply wounds every part of the person, including our relationships. Even though our relationship with God is spiritual in nature, it too suffers. If you are struggling with your relationship with your heavenly Father, please know that you have nothing to feel guilty about. God understands the pain you've endured. He understands that you're angry, afraid, and feeling distant.

So many things change — physical, emotional, and spiritual — when sexual abuse happens. Our faith suffers; trust (in earthly beings as well as divine) is deeply affected. The good news is that you can feel hope again. You can feel whole again. Certain relationships that may have been affected throughout the course of your abuse can be rebuilt and repaired, and that includes your relationship with your Creator.

My relationship with God was deeply affected after my rape. Not only was I hurt by someone I trusted, but he was also supposed to be someone who reflected God. Of course, the actions of the priest who hurt me reflected God in no way, shape, or form, but it took me a long time to fully process and understand that. I had a hard time accepting God as an all-loving Father, and I struggled to trust him for a long time. This is something a lot of abuse victims struggle with, whether their abuser was a priest, a family member, an acquaintance, or a stranger.

Spiritually, I became hollow, struggling to see God, a part of me not caring to find him — if he was even around. More than once, I had people say to me, "You just need to pray more! You're not praying enough!" As though my suffering was caused by a lack of faith or a lack of prayer!

Right now I want to reassure you: whatever kind of abuse you endured, you did not deserve it, and it did not happen because of any fault of your own. You do not need to feel guilty or ashamed if you don't feel God's love or if you don't feel anything during prayer — or if you have a hard time praying. Emotionally, spending long periods of time praying or reflecting on your faith is going to be difficult and may even feel quite burdensome. I talked a bit about how trauma alters the brain, and one of the brain's defenses against abuse (whether real or perceived) is to "shut down" feelings, even good feelings. Trauma lives in the front of our minds, and there will be days, especially early in your healing journey, when it will be overwhelming. Other days, thanks to the brain's defense mechanisms, you might not think about it as much. Healing truly is a roller-coaster ride of thoughts and emotions! My advice: Start small and just do what you can. God believes in you, and he isn't giving up on you, so don't worry about that.

Some of you may be wondering, what does it mean to pray? Your immediate thought may be particular prayers such as the Hail Mary, the Our Father, and the Glory Be. While memorized words such as these are indeed prayers, prayer can move beyond the prayers of a book. Every time we talk to God or open our hearts to listening to his voice (in an interior sense) — whether it's done formally or informally — we are praying. Saint Thérèse, the Little Flower, once said, "For me, prayer is a surge of the heart; it is a simple look turned toward heaven, it is a cry of recognition and of love, embracing both trial and joy." What a beautiful (and accurate) definition of what prayer is!

There are different kinds of prayer and different ways in which to pray. First, let's talk about the different types of prayer. The *Catechism of the Catholic Church* tells us that there are five forms: blessing, petition, intercession, thanksgiving, and praise:

> Because God blesses the human heart, it can in return bless him who is the source of every blessing.
>
> Forgiveness, the quest for the Kingdom, and every true need are objects of the prayer of petition.
>
> Prayer of intercession consists in asking on behalf of

another. It knows no boundaries and extends to one's enemies.

Every joy and suffering, every event and need can become the matter for thanksgiving which, sharing in that of Christ, should fill one's whole life: "Give thanks in all circumstances" *(1 Thes 5:18).*

Prayer of praise is entirely disinterested and rises to God, lauds him, and gives him glory for his own sake, quite beyond what he has done, but simply because HE IS. (2645–2649)

Reflecting on my own prayer life, I can look back and see how it has changed and grown. Personally, I spent a long time praying prayers of petition (I asked God for help — during and after the rape). Over time, as I gradually accepted God's gift of gratitude more and more, I additionally began praying prayers of thanksgiving. Over time, prayers of praise and blessing came easier and, eventually, prayers of intercession. Nowadays I'd say there's much more of a balance of the different types of prayer in my life, though one may seem to appear more than others, depending on what I'm going through at any given time.

No matter where you are in your relationship with God, I encourage you to keep striving to take the path toward him. Keep the channels of communication open, and allow his great graces to flow into your soul. What are some ways you can do that? Well, now that we've discussed the different types of prayer, here are some ideas on how to pray.

Meditation

In mentioning meditation, I'm not talking about all that Eastern spirituality stuff (for further clarification about a Catholic view of meditation and prayer, please read *Catechism of the Catholic Church* 2705–2708). The Catholic idea of meditation is very different and usually involves doing some sort of spiritual reading (for example, the Bible) and then reflecting upon it. In other words, how is God speaking to me through what I've just read? This is different from just plowing through a book in an academic sense. Ignatian-style meditation and *lectio divina* are two methods of Catholic meditation that you might want to learn more about.

Hymns

Saint Augustine said, "He who sings prays twice." There are lots of beautiful traditional Catholic hymns and contemporary Christian songs to choose from, and they are all different forms of prayer — hymns of blessing, petition, intercession, thanksgiving, and praise. Listening to, singing along with, and making music can connect us more deeply to the Scriptures and can speak to our minds and hearts in a powerful way.

Silent Prayer

Sometimes we just need silence — no books, no music, and no interruptions. During that silent time (whether at home, outside, or in church), we can either speak to God silently from our hearts or just sit in his presence and listen to what he has to tell us. Eucharistic adoration is a great way to do this.

Formal Prayer

By "formal prayer," I'm talking about prayers you might read in a prayer book, such as novenas, litanies, and the prayers many of us are familiar with, including the Hail Mary, the Our Father, and the Saint Michael prayer. These prayers can be especially helpful during times when you're running on empty and you just don't know what to say. The repetitive nature of many prayers can also be quite soothing and help to calm an anxious mind because of the concentration they require.

Personal Prayer

Though formal prayers are wonderful, sometimes we do well simply to put ourselves into the presence of God and talk to him. What can you talk to him about? Anything! Even though he already knows everything, like any loving Father he loves when we bring him our thoughts, desires, concerns, praise, gratitude, and so forth. In the words of Saint Alphonsus Liguori, "Acquire the habit of speaking to God as if you were alone with him, familiarly and with confidence and love, as to the dearest and most loving of friends." There is absolutely nothing we can tell God that he doesn't already know or that he won't understand. No matter how ashamed or embarrassed we may feel, God loves us. You don't have to sit for hours at a time. You don't even have to say anything. Your prayer can be as simple as sitting quietly and telling Jesus to take what's in your heart. Again, Eucharistic adoration is a great way to do this. Sometimes I have specific things to ask or pray about; sometimes I just want to praise God and thank him for all his blessings; but sometimes my brain is just so muddled that I can't put together a coherent thought. All I can do is sit quietly and open my heart to his love and grace. Just be sure to leave some time for listening to him speaking deeply within your heart.

No one on earth can boast about having a perfect relationship with God. However, the more we are aware of him through prayer, Scripture, and the sacraments, the closer we are brought to him and the more fully we want to live the life he is inspiring us to live. This is especially true of the greatest gift Jesus Christ left us on earth — the gift of his Body, Blood, Soul, and Divinity in the Sacrament of the Holy Eucharist. As a Catholic, I believe that that little white host is more than just bread. It is Jesus himself. The True Presence is something that a lot of people (Catholics and non-Catholics alike) struggle to understand and believe, but as the *Catechism* tells us, "the Eucharist is 'the source and summit of the Christian life.' ... For in the blessed Eucharist is contained the whole spiritual good of the Church, namely Christ himself, our Pasch" (1324). When I consider how far I've come in my life, I can say without hesitation that I would not be here if it weren't for the Eucharist.

I assure you, I felt nothing when I received Jesus in the sacraments. As a matter of fact, I fought my parents about going to church after my rape and resented them for making me go. For a long time, we attended a different Catholic Church in our town so that I was not constantly being faced with certain triggers. However, I definitely still struggled to enter any church, not just the one I was raped at. Just opening the door caused me physical pain and torment — my head would pound as if it was going to burst, and my stomach twisted so horribly that I felt sick. Emotionally, I would shut down and allow my mind to wander. Focusing on the great gift before me was impossible.

Whether I felt anything or not, Christ was still coming to me and giving me grace. Whether I said the prayers of the Mass with feeling or whether I said them at all, God heard what was in my heart. He met me where I was and never gave up on me. Looking back, I understand that what my parents did for me by making me attend Mass with them was a gift. God gives us grace when we pray, but he especially gives us grace when we go to Mass. Maybe church was the last place I wanted to be at that time, but I was gaining unseen strength, courage, perseverance — all of the beautiful gifts mentioned in this devotional. I attribute this to the greatest gift Jesus Christ left us here on earth — the gift of his most precious Body and Blood in the Sacrament of the Holy Eucharist. I was not alone, and this was something I came to realize over time.

Is entering a church easy now that I'm an adult and twenty years have passed since my rape? I wouldn't call it easy, no. I'm able to enter a church without feeling ill or anxious, but I sometimes have to fight an interior battle. If, for whatever reason, I don't think I can handle being at a particular church, my family simply attends Mass at a different church on that day.

The fact of the matter is, no matter what kind of trauma we have endured in our lives, we cannot heal alone. We need the help of other human beings (whenever possible), and methods of healing such as therapy are extremely helpful, but we need God's divine help especially. Saint John Paul II said, "Prayer is in fact the recognition of our limits and our dependence: we come from God, we are of God, and to God we return." We are merely human, and God is divine. We need to rely on him. Otherwise, the road to healing is going to be a whole lot harder and longer, and we may come to see giving up as easier than continuing on.

APPENDIX II

The Reality of Sexual Grooming

If you or a loved one or a friend has been affected by sexual abuse, I am truly sorry for your pain and suffering. No one deserves to go through that. Perhaps my words and tears change nothing, but I do pray that you find hope, healing, and peace through the power of Jesus Christ.

You are not alone! Make no mistake: Sexual abuse goes on everywhere — in schools, in churches (of all religions), in businesses, on sports teams, in families, and just about anywhere else you can think of. It affects males, females, young, and old. Never fall into the trap of thinking that it affects only one particular sex or age. Sexual abuse knows no age limit or racial or religious barrier. The conversation about the prevalence of sexual abuse continues to grow, and for good reason. Sexual abuse was once hush-hush, but our culture is becoming more aware of the issue and not only finding ways to help survivors, but also trying to find ways to prevent such abuse. There is no magical solution or cure, but I can tell you that we need to pray and turn back to God. When a world turns away from God and instead turns to evil, bad things are bound to follow. Sexual abuse has become a despicable, almost routine evil in this world, and, rest assured, Our Lord and Our Blessed Mother are angry. I get goosebumps whenever I hear the passage from the Gospel of Matthew:

> At that time the disciples came to Jesus, saying, "Who is the greatest in the kingdom of heaven?" And calling to him a child, he put him in the midst of them, and said, "Truly, I say to you, unless you turn and become like children, you will never enter the kingdom of heaven. Whoever humbles himself like this child, he is the greatest in the kingdom of heaven. Whoever receives one such child in my name receives me; but whoever causes one of these

little ones who believe in me to sin, it would be better for him to have a great millstone fastened round his neck and to be drowned in the depth of the sea. Woe to the world for temptations to sin! For it is necessary that temptations come, but woe to the man by whom the temptation comes!" (18:1–7)

Our Lord's words make one's skin crawl. Imagine what terrible punishment awaits those who corrupt the minds of the innocent, for Jesus to say such harsh words. I can almost see the fire coming from Our Lord's eyes as he spoke this. He makes it quite clear how precious the innocent are to him, and so, while forgiveness is always offered to those who repent of hurting others, those who do not repent have a heavy price to pay. God always offers mercy to those who have sinned. However, forgiveness comes through their true contrition and atonement. Many priests who have been guilty of sexual abuse admitted to their sins and perhaps said they were sorry, but, once relocated, they assaulted again. This is not true contrition.

One of the most misunderstood and often ignored aspects of sexual abuse is that of sexual grooming. What is sexual grooming? In short, it is the process by which an abuser slowly gains the trust of a victim. The predator gains an individual's trust and determines how much access he or she has to the victim. Once the predator can have that access, he or she desensitizes the victim to touch and manipulates the relationship. In an overwhelming number of sexual abuse cases, the abuser waits for the "right" victim and slowly grooms that person. A person of any age or sex can be groomed. Predators can be anyone, male or female — a friend, a family member, a teacher, a coach, a clergyman, or a stranger who slowly seeks out a relationship with a potential victim. Grooming can happen anywhere: in person, online, in a school, at a church, on the playground, and so forth.

In my own case of sexual abuse, my rapist took advantage of the fact that I was a somewhat naive, innocent, awkward fifteen-year-old girl who was seeking advice from him. He slowly got to know me. He took advantage of the fact that I was almost always alone when I was working in the parish rectory on Saturday afternoons. He became familiar with my schedule, he figured out who would be around, and so forth. The physical touching didn't start right away; it was only after several weeks and, even then, the first touches were seemingly innocent (brief touches to the shoulder or back gradually became longer touches, which led to caresses of the arm, eventually leading to more invasive, more inappropriate touches). During the time I was being abused, he would often insert himself into my conversations with friends after Mass. If I ever walked off alone during parish events, he would almost always eventually follow.

A predator manipulates not only the victim, but also the victim's family or people around the victim. In my case, my rapist was charming, helpful, cheerful, and well-liked by my parish community. Even after I came forward with my story and faced him in a trial, he maintained his innocence and continued to charm parishioners, many of whom helped to fund his defense.

Predators allow people to see what they want them to see. They hide behind a mask, and there's a monster behind that mask. Unfortunately, especially in today's world, it is important for parents and caregivers in particular to research and learn about sexual grooming. Learning about grooming can be very helpful for abuse survivors too, because it can help to alleviate some of the guilt and shame that all victims feel.

Just remember that if you have been a victim of any kind of abuse, you did not deserve it, and it was not your fault.

APPENDIX III

Sexual Abuse Resources

If you or a loved one are suffering or have suffered from sexual abuse, you may be wondering where to go or whom you can talk to.

First of all, you are not alone. Chances are, you are not your abuser's only victim. Even if you are the first, there will likely be more victims in the future. I understand that there are often various factors involved in whether a victim chooses to go to authorities or to report the abuse. However, if you are able to, I encourage you to report the crime as soon as possible and seek psychological and spiritual help.

The following is a list of several resources to help put you on the right track. Any one of these resources can help.

1. **Call 911 or go to your local police department** and ask to speak with someone who specializes in sexual assault. Many police departments have a special unit or, at the very least, individuals specially trained to handle sexual assault cases.

2. **Sexual Abuse Hotlines**
    - National Sexual Assault Hotline: 800.656.HOPE
    - National Child Abuse Hotline: 800.422.4453

3. **Informative Websites**
    - Rape, Abuse & Incest National Network: www.rainn.org
    - National Federation for Catholic Youth Ministry (NFCYM): www.nfcym.org/youthprotection
    - Ruth Institute — provides research and education tools to support individuals affected by the sexual revolution: www .ruthinstitute.org
    - Made in His Image — a nonprofit providing hope and healing for female survivors of abuse: www.madeinhisimage.org

4. **For Survivors of Clerical Abuse**

   If you or a loved one has been a victim of clerical abuse, the United States Conference of Catholic Bishops online has a thorough list of victim assistance coordinators by diocese or archdiocese: http://www.usccb.org/issues-and-action/child -and-youth-protection/victim-assistance.cfm

5. **Psychotherapy**

   A good therapist is a crucial element in the healing process. Whenever possible, I recommend finding a Catholic therapist. You can search by state at catholictherapists.com.

6. **Even if your insurance is a factor, call and speak with a therapist anyway.** Depending on your situation, your therapy may be eligible for coverage from your diocese, archdiocese, or wherever the abuse occurred.

ABOUT THE AUTHOR

Faith Hakesley is a wife, homeschooling mother of three, and blogger. Over the course of her life, she has overcome many traumas, including rape by a Catholic priest and the death of a brother, and has lived through cancer as well as a serious heart condition.

In 2008, she was one of five victims of clerical abuse to meet privately with Pope Benedict XVI during his trip to Washington, D.C. Since that meeting, she has been passionate about sharing her personal story of healing in order to offer hope, healing, and peace to those who are suffering. She seeks to break the stigmas associated with trauma and to encourage others to find hope through their faith.

She and her family live in Massachusetts. Visit her website, www.faithhakesley.com, for more information or to connect with her on social media.